Contents

006
Laurie Melia & Rod Flynn
BASSENDEAN, WA

014
Rick Hayward & Emily Devers
RED HILL, QLD

024
Geordie Malone & Eartha Smith
NEWCASTLE, NSW

034
Candice Carlin
& Murray Cronin
HOBART, TAS

042
Abbey Rich
BRUNSWICK WEST, VIC

050
Danni Harris & Alec Hall
KENSINGTON, SA

058
Eileen Braybrook
& Stefan Delatovic
BRUNSWICK, VIC

066
Inner-city Neighbours
CAMPERDOWN, NSW

076
Hayley & Chadd Kessner
CATTERICK, WA

084
Emma Byrnes & Pete Barrett
FITZROY NORTH, VIC

094
Kyra Bartley & David Collins
ST PETERS, NSW

100
Rachel Burke & Thomas Lynch
STAFFORD, QLD

110
Steph Hughes & Mia Mala McDonald
BRUNSWICK, VIC

116
Dawn & Andrew Lindsay
MELBOURNE, VIC

126
FLOWERS, TEXTURES &
OTHER PRETTY THINGS

144
Mabel & Ivy Windred-Wornes
NORTHCOTE, VIC

150
Josh Barnes &
Emma Schuberg Barnes
KATOOMBA, NSW

160
Patrick Floyd Meade
VENUS BAY, VIC

168
Sam James, Emma Finneran
& Matt Bromhead
SURRY HILLS, NSW

176
Katia Carletti & Rohan Fraser
NAILSWORTH, SA

184
Nicholson Street Studios
BRUNSWICK EAST, VIC

194
Ophelia Mikkelson & Ryder Jones
TAIRUA, NZ

202
Alex Bennett & Tina Helm
CAMPBELLS CREEK, VIC

212
CREATIVE SPACES IN ASIA

214
Allpress x SPACES Partnership
TOKYO

218
Ly Yeow
SINGAPORE

226
Jae-sun You
SEOUL

234
Nataly Lee & Euan Gray
PHNOM PENH

242
Azumi Sakata
TOKYO

250
Jordan Marzuki
JAKARTA

There's no place like home.
There's no place like home.
There's no place like home.

DOROTHY IN *THE WIZARD OF OZ*

Laurie Melia & Rod Flynn
live with their dog, Duke, in
Bassendean, WA. Laurie is a ceramic
artist; Rod is a gardener.

WORDS KATE VELING PHOTOGRAPHS RACHEL WOODS

The house Laurie Melia and her husband, Rod Flynn, live in is on top of a hill. "All the windows are above the fence line," she says. "We can see right to the bottom of our street from the kitchen." That's just one of the things they love about their place in Bassendean, on the outskirts of Perth. The fact that the two of them, along with their dog, Duke (who does an excellent job as a security guard and excavator), have more than enough room to do all the things they want to do is another bonus. Over the past four years, Laurie and Rod have been in the process of making the three-bedroom cottage completely theirs.

It has a picket fence and all the usual features you'd expect to find in an old house – high ceilings, jarrah floorboards, front porch and a fireplace in the lounge room (which sadly no longer works). At some point, previous owners renovated the kitchen and bathroom and knocked down a wall between the kitchen and living area.

"I love that it's small enough to be cosy but also feels quite spacious," says Laurie. The original features mean it had character even before they got their hands on it. "And it lets us get away with being less restrained with our decorating, which is handy."

There is no one particular style, she says. "I guess my personal style has a bit more creative clutter to it, whereas Rod likes things more minimalist and uniform. I also have no restraint with colour, and he likes mainly brown and grey."

That could be a bit of a problem in some households, but not for this pair. "Laurie just does what she wants, but really our styles aren't that dissimilar," Rod says. "I guess

both of us see things we like or make things ourselves, and then find a place for them."

There was, however, one piece that created some debate between them – the painting above the fireplace. Even though she concedes it's slightly too small for the space, Laurie loves it. At first Rod wasn't keen on putting it on display, let alone in the most prominent position in the house. But, he says, "It belonged to Laurie's grandparents and is therefore special to her, so it stayed. Over time I got used to it and now I actually quite like it."

Elsewhere, Laurie's ceramics decorate mantles, shelves and table tops all over the house, and Rod has made a fair bit of the furniture from recycled timber, including a built-in bookshelf in the living room and a wine rack near the front door. "We have both contributed to a lot of what is in our home," says Laurie. "There are lots of references around the place to things we like and places we've been." Things like the *Back to the Future* series above the bar – a reference to one of Rod's favourite movies – and a framed picture of Kevin Costner in *Waterworld*. "I'm a huge Kevin Costner fan," says Laurie.

From her home studio, Laurie creates small batches of her ceramics – sculpting, painting, glazing, firing and photographing them to upload to her Etsy store, Yellow Tree, where they sell out within minutes. She's known for her hands flipping the bird, odd little characters, ceramic jewellery, trinket trays and a hotchpotch of ornaments and vases. There are her Nicolas Cage and Bill Murray cushions, too. "They are two of my favourite actors, with expressive faces that were fun to draw," says Laurie. "I did have a Kevin Costner series, but they weren't very popular."

Left page, below left: The painting above the fireplace used to belong to Laurie's grandparents; Rod wasn't too keen on it at first.

That old adage, "A place for everything and everything in its place", does not apply at our place.

←

When she's working, Laurie doesn't usually get stuck in the studio for too long. "I often branch out into the kitchen, and on packing days there's not a spare surface left," she says. "The main pro of working from home is that I can work any time I want. Inspiration doesn't always hit at the same time of day and I like that I can get straight to work on an idea as soon as it pops into my head. The cons are that during very busy times I never really switch off because all my work is sitting there right under my nose."

With new pieces being created on a regular basis, Laurie shifts things around quite a lot. A piece might sit on a shelf for a while before she decides to sell it. "That old adage, 'A place for everything and everything in its place' does not apply at our house," she says. "I'm talking small level changes, though – rearranging mantles and shelves, changing pictures around and adding baskets. I have an obsession with baskets. I'm literally at the point of buying baskets for my baskets."

Larger scale changes to the house have been done by Rod. As a gardener and musician he has taken charge of the outdoor areas and converted the garage into a music room, where he can hang out, play guitar and turn up the volume without worrying about noise complaints from the neighbours.

"I lived in a couple of share houses before Laurie and I got together so there was always a room of some sort dedicated to jamming, but this is the nicest by far," says Rod of his custom-made music room. It's properly soundproofed and definitely has his less

colourful style about it in the way of decoration. There are his instruments, drum kits and desk in there, band posters on the wall and all sorts of amps and other musical equipment, but that's about it.

As for the garden, it's "100 per cent Rod and always looks amazing", says Laurie. When they moved in, it consisted of a little bit of lawn, some agapanthus and a row of rose bushes along the fence. "I kind of hate agapanthus so the first thing I did was rip them out," says Rod. "I built a raised vegetable patch in the sunniest corner of the property, planted fruit trees along the fence line and, on Laurie's insistence, a bougainvillea down the back of the garden."

Over time he's added a row of pear trees along the front for privacy and filled up the garden beds around the trees with succulents and natives as well as lots of pot plants and a water feature. "I spend a lot of time in the garden tending to everything I've planted," he says. "It looks great and it's probably my favourite place to be."

Even though they've already been in the house for four years now, it still throws up the odd surprise. One night after a few drinks, they became curious about what looked like a trapdoor in the kitchen floorboards. They prised up the boards with a crowbar and discovered an underground room. "It was littered with old cork cigarette butts and packets of Bex, so that was pretty exciting," says Laurie. "I love to think about all the previous incarnations our house has had and the people who have called it home." •

Left page, below left: Laurie works out of her tiny home studio, making small batches of ceramics that she sells online.

Rick Hayward & Emily Devers
live in a studio in Red Hill, Brisbane.
They work together on illustration,
signage, & other bits & bobs.

WORDS KATE VELING PHOTOGRAPHS NATALIE MCCOMAS

When you've been living in the back of a troop carrier for three months with two bikes and a dog, even the smallest apartment can seem like the Taj Mahal. That was the case when Rick Hayward and Emily Devers returned to Brisbane after an extended East Coast road trip and inspected a very modest one-room studio in Red Hill. The woman who owned the house, and lived upstairs, was an illustrator, and the studio used to be her workspace. They decided it was the perfect place at the perfect time, and put their case forward to become the new tenants.

"We were a bit nervous, though, because she was a self-proclaimed cat person and we have a dog," says Rick, referring to their third family member, Peter Allen, the Tenterfield terrier. "We thought that could be a deal breaker, but he's a very cute little dog and she loves him. We had a one-month trial period and he totally won her over."

They have been living in their little studio for almost four years now. Neither of them are Brisbane natives. Rick is from Coffs Harbour, NSW, and migrated north after doing his apprenticeship in sign-writing on the Gold Coast. Emily is originally from Melbourne and moved to Queensland's capital after finishing high school on the Sunshine Coast.

Their original plan was to stay in the studio for only a few months. It was never a conscious decision to put down roots in Brisbane. "We talk about moving away to Northern NSW or the hinterland but it feels pretty good here at the moment," says Emily.

Rick and Emily are also known as Frank & Mimi, a studio specialising in signage, murals, fit-outs and other bits and pieces that combine traditional sign painting techniques with contemporary design and execution. In an industry where digital is dominant, they've gone for the handmade.

When they met six years ago, Emily was completing a degree in fine arts. In 2011 she was asked to contribute to a local exhibition and pitched the idea of doing a live mural with her partner. That was their first

collaboration and, to this day, new clients still reference that artwork as the kind of thing they'd like. Nowadays, Frank & Mimi's designs, murals and signs adorn the walls and facades of many Brisbane buildings and popular venues.

When they first moved in to the studio, Rick and Emily were working from home. "That didn't work at all," says Emily. "It was too tight. We'd wake up and be looking at our work."

To say the studio is cosy is a bit of an understatement, yet it doesn't feel cramped. The kitchen, dining area, lounge and bedroom all inhabit the same space, with a toilet and shower in a hidden nook behind a beaded curtain. There's also a small walk-in wardrobe for storage and clothes.

Living in such a small space has taught the pair a lot about simplicity, quality over quantity and living consciously. Books and bikes are the two things they find hard to limit (at one stage Rick had nine bikes in the studio), but all other items are carefully considered before any purchase is made.

While they love the way it's set up now, it took a few goes to get it right. "We've definitely changed things around, moving the bed regularly and re-organising the kitchen," says Rick. "The beauty of living a simple existence is that it doesn't take much to make it feel fresh again."

Moving the business out of home was probably the biggest change they've made. Fortunately, they found the perfect location for it in one of Red Hill's oldest buildings, The Foundry Studios. The venue once housed a brass foundry but is now shared by a collective of Brisbane artisans, artists and makers, including a sustainable architectural firm, furniture makers, a rooftop beehive business and a bonafide blacksmith.

The people they share the space with have become friends, too, and Emily says the bonus is that many of their mates live within a few blocks. "The creative community in Brisbane is ultra-connected, and ultra-supportive. For now, I'm the most at home I've ever felt."

Left page: Some of the furniture in the studio comes from Rick and Emily's friends, including their bed, which was made by Talty Sargent.

Everything in our little home has significance and meaning, but is by no measure curated.

Conveniently, The Foundry Studios are a 15-minute walk from their home and their route takes them through the park, so their commute consists of a twice-daily stroll with Pete, their pooch, who hangs out at work with them, too. "It's a nice way to clear your mind for the day, and then at the end of the day as well," says Rick.

Both agree that having work and home separate is good for their mental state. "We develop concepts by responding to briefs every day for work, and coming home for us is solace from this process," says Rick. "Everything in our little home has significance and meaning, but is by no measure curated. Things have come together very naturally in here, as it's important to us that our minds can feel relaxed when we're in the space."

They've furnished their living quarters with a mix of second-hand finds and considered purchases. Textiles from Emily's recent trip to Morocco adorn the lounge and bed and her jewellery is displayed around the place. But their favourite items in their home are things their friends have made by hand.

Their bed (which has storage space underneath) and coffee table are both custom-made by Talty Sargent, studio mates at The Foundry, and a print from another Foundry friend, Shilo Engelbrecht, hangs above their desk.

The long table and filing cabinet in the centre of the space were there when they moved in. The two pieces are bolted together and are a permanent fixture, but that suits the couple well. In fact, it's Emily's favourite feature in the studio apartment. "We do everything at that table. We prepare food on it, we've had long table feasts around it, we create artwork

at it and host visitors and converse around it. It's seen a lot of life."

Apart from rearranging their belongings, Rick and Emily have made minimal changes to their space. They recently swapped the grey '80s venetian blinds in the kitchen for timber ones, which has been a huge improvement and added a lot of warmth to the light coming through the window.

The pair say that living and working in such close proximity has strengthened their relationship in ways they didn't anticipate. "We make an effort to be open with each other if we're feeling frustrated about something, and to realise that those frustrations are not necessarily directed at each other," says Rick. "We try to catch ourselves before it starts affecting our dynamic. And we also have a little diffuser with a tail."

"Also, I think living in such a small space has been really awesome for that because you can't just go and stew on something in another room, or kick up a fuss and then go hide in the study," adds Emily. "You have to confront any issues right away. We do things on our own, too. Rick makes time to go out and ride at the trails and I'll go and hang with the girls. If we didn't have those things it would probably get a bit intense."

While they both agree that more natural light would be ideal, there's really not much they can find to fault in their current living arrangement. "Just having our own garden I miss – it's been a trade-off," says Emily. "We realise those things will come in the future, but for now we're just making the most of it. We just take it all on the chin, as one day we'll be living in a stone cottage on Tasmanian acreage!" •

Left page: Rick and Emily used to work from home, but now are part of a collective space within walking distance from their studio.

Geordie Malone & Eartha Smith
live with their children, Howlin'
Jack Watt & Emmylou Fox Malone,
in Newcastle, NSW. Geordie is a
leatherworker, Eartha is a vintage
collector, & they own a shop.

WORDS LETA KEENS PHOTOGRAPHS SASKIA WILSON

There's plenty of old stuff in Geordie Malone and Eartha Smith's place. Lots to look at, and most of it has a story attached to it. It would be easy, however, to overlook one thing in a display unit at the top of the stairs – a tiny little glass bottle, cracked all over, a bit dirty looking inside, and all they have left from one chapter in their lives.

"It still has smoke in it," says Eartha, explaining that she found it in the ashes after Morrow Park, an old Newcastle bowling club and arts hub, burnt down. It's where she and Geordie met, and where both of them had been living at one stage. When Morrow Park went up in flames, Eartha, who has a vintage clothes business, had all her stock there. "I lost everything – hundreds of dresses and bags."

After that, they lived in "a kooky three-storey warehouse" for a while. The prospect of moving into a normal house was a bit scary, but with two kids, it was time to live a slightly more traditional life. "If we're in the suburbs, we still want to be weird," says Eartha. As soon as they found their house in Georgetown, they knew it was all going to be OK. "This was weird, and we could make it weirder."

For a start, there is the bell – the classic Avon Lady ding dong variety. "We're getting the house – it's got a doorbell!" Eartha recalls thinking. And virtually every room had a different wallpaper – wild designs from the '70s – and a bathroom with the lairiest tiles you could imagine. When it was open for inspection, people were talking about ripping it all apart. "We were getting offended by what everyone was saying about 'our' house, and it wasn't even our house," says Geordie.

The old lady who'd been living there had brought up her family in it – her children, all getting on themselves, put the house on the market after she died. "We had a chat with them and when they were telling us about their mum and all her '60s outfits, they could see how excited I was getting," says Eartha. "I think they were hoping we'd get the place."

They did, and as they've got to know people in the area, they've discovered a whole

bunch of houses nearby have similarly crazy wallpaper to theirs, although not in quite such vast quantities – the neighbours were all friends and most probably shopped together. They've also found out that it's a really friendly neighbourhood – everyone helps each other out and there's a lot of chatting over fences.

When they moved in, the family had left them a brilliant blue bottle, which is now part of the collection on the cabinet in the living area. There was a "spectacular" pants suit that their mum had made, as well, plus a drawer full of old fabrics. And a photo of how the house looked originally – a fairly standard 1930s brick bungalow. In the '70s, instead of adding to it by putting on a top storey, as most people would, the whole house was jacked up and a lower level added. All the lovely old windows were ripped out and replaced by '70s bay windows; the odd column was added, too. From outside, it's impossible to recognise anything '30s about the place.

Downstairs, as well as Geordie and Eartha's bedroom, which used to be the rumpus room, there's a granny flat where Eartha's mother and her husband are living at the moment. Her mum is in charge of the garden, which has a great vegetable patch, and even helped Howlin' tag one corner of the shed with a slightly sinister looking smiley face. "She told him he could draw a face, and that would be his happy place," says Eartha. Her mum, however, is not into Eartha's growing collection of garden statues. "There's a shop I go to where the woman knows exactly what I like," says Eartha. "When she found the frog loveseat, I was like, 'Yes!'. She says she has a hip-high possum I have to check out. Mum says no possums."

When Geordie and Eartha and the children moved in, they camped downstairs for a month while Geordie and his dad "went to town trying to get everything fixed". That meant ripping up carpets and sanding floors, getting rid of the heavy curtains, stripping a bit of boring stripy wallpaper, painting ceilings and any bare walls, painting the floor of Emmylou's playroom (which used to be the back porch) and getting gas and new wiring installed.

→

←

They were even given some "cool old doors" by one of their neighbours – they were just the right size for the downstairs bedroom. One thing that still might get an update one day is the kitchen, with its saloon doors, but no one's in any hurry. "It's tiny, and problematic if there's more than one person in it," says Geordie. "But for me, doing the cooking, it's like a workspace in a café."

Once the painting was done, the living area, with its white walls, looked a bit on the dull side. The only way to liven it up, reckoned Eartha, was with wallpaper, and she found a beauty in a Danish online vintage shop. "I pretty well did everything in the house but that," says Geordie. "I couldn't risk ruining it – there's a real art to putting it up." Buying the wallpaper and getting it hung was by far the most expensive thing in the house, says Eartha, but definitely worth it. The couch, an eBay find from Castlemaine in Victoria, probably came a close second, and was not a great decision because of the kids, she says. "I didn't want to be one of those people who said, 'Don't go near the couch.' Once it had been vomited on a few times, though, I got over that."

For Geordie, doing up the house came pretty naturally. "I've made things my entire life," he says. "As a kid, I had my own work area, and would get up, go in there and see what I could start nailing together." After he left school, he lived and worked with a mate's uncle who was a carpenter-builder, and later did a cabinet-making course.

He's also been in a few bands, and while on the road, got bored by not being able to make anything. He wanted something small enough to work on in the back of a van, and that's when a friend showed him the basics of leatherwork. It's not such a stretch from

carpentry, he says. "Once you can make stuff out of one material, you can switch to other materials quite easily."

The first things he made were a belt and a tiny wallet; since then, he's built up quite a repertoire of bags, belts, wallets and even custom-made cases for industrial use. At first, he made things for friends, then moved on to a market stall, which he still has. Two years ago, he and Eartha set up their shop, Hide and Seeker, in Islington, a quick bike ride from home. Eartha had been selling vintage clothes at markets, and also sold them online until she got sick of all the admin involved. For her, second-hand clothes have always been part of life. "Mum and Dad had four kids and no money," she says. "We were hippies who lived out on an island near Forster. Mum took us to op shops which was really embarrassing when I was young – I'd worry that people would see me. But I got into it myself when I was in year nine, and that was it."

Their little shop, with displays of Geordie's leatherwork and racks of Eartha's clothes, many of which come from Japan, has a good sized work area out the back where Geordie can work but still keep an eye on what's going on. The shop was an architect's office directly before they moved in, and to give it the kind of look they were after, they papered one wall in vintage wallpaper. Soon after they moved in, a woman came in to order a custom-made photo album. "It turned out she'd grown up upstairs, and her grandpa was a shoemaker and leatherworker right here in this shop," says Geordie.

Eventually, they may expand, but for now they're happy where they are, doing what they do. "You see people around Newcastle wearing one of my dresses or with one of Geordie's bags and I love it," says Eartha. •

Left page, below right:
The frog loveseat, bought
at a local shop, is part
of Eartha's collection of
garden statues.

Candice Carlin & Murray Cronin

live in Hobart with their two cats &
a dog. Candice is a photographer
& graphic designer; Murray is a
secondary school teacher.

WORDS KOREN HELBIG PHOTOGRAPHS CANDICE CARLIN

**Candice Carlin and Murray Cronin never
officially decided to move in together. Having
grown up in the same small New South Wales
town of Nelson Bay, they started dating while
still living with their respective folks, then
began sharing digs while overseas on a
year-long adventure in the UK.**

When they came back to Australia in 2012
and Murray landed a teaching job in rural
Tasmania, giving island life a go together
seemed like a no-brainer. Plus, they were
offered teachers' housing, and later moved
to the cheap rent utopia that is Launceston.
Says Candice: "You'd go to an inspection and
be the only one there. They'd say, 'Do you
want it?' And you'd be like, 'Um... yeah!'"

Buying in Tassie was a different story
altogether, however. Murray had been keeping
a casual eye on the market before they moved
to Hobart in early 2015 and got serious about
the search. Even then, it was almost a year
before they found what they were looking
for. Promising places were often snapped up
before they hit the market, while others were
just downright dodgy. "I remember one with
some vines growing inside," Candice says.

They struck gold with the place they eventually
bought. It's exceptionally well built, because
the bloke who designed and constructed it
in the 1940s was a builder, intent on crafting
the perfect home for his little family. Case
in point: the house has a fully functioning
laundry chute, which Candice and Murray only
stumbled upon weeks after moving in. "It's
under the bathroom sink, and the laundry's
under the house in the garage, so you just put
your dirty clothes under the basin and they
go straight downstairs. It's the biggest luxury
ever," Candice says. They also immediately
fell in love with their home's mid-century
"cool *Jetsons* vibe", especially the sandstone
fireplace and steel-frame windows, the likes of
which aren't made anymore. "The house has a
really interesting floor plan, too," Candice says.
"You walk in and it's a long hallway to the left
and right, so you can go one way to the sleeping
and bathroom end and the other way to the
living room and kitchen. It's a really clever
design, a big L-shape."

What's more, few things needed immediate
attention, aside from a new coat of paint
for the one bedroom that had been painted
a weird shade of dark blue. "We're not
home-renovating people. I like old stuff and
everything, but I don't really know how to fix
things," Candice says, although she admits
they made an exception for the blocky old
wooden table they discovered in their garage.
"It had paint all over it and was covered in
spiders when we pulled it out, which was
kind of gross. But we couldn't be bothered
buying a table so we got this big bit of board
from Bunnings and just plonked it on, nailed
it down. So that's the kitchen table; it's
probably about 60 years old."

At some stage they'll pull up the kitchen's
'90s vinyl and the bedrooms' "nana carpet",
too, mainly because they know mint condition
Tasmanian oak floorboards are hiding
underneath. "We're only the third owners
of this house, so we know they haven't been
knocked around," Candice says.

Murray and Candice share their place with
two Norwegian forest cats, named Forest
("We went for the obvious name," Candice says)
and Orla, as well as an Irish setter, Oslo, who
thinks the bedroom is his kennel. The moves
they made around Tassie before settling in
Hobart were an exercise in minimalism when
it comes to other belongings. "At the start,
you think, 'I like this a bit, I'll keep it.' But by
the end, it's like, 'I don't care, I'll throw away
everything! I wish I didn't own anything!'"

Only possessions they really loved survived
the cull, such as a babushka doll Candice's
nan brought back from a holiday in Russia.
"She gave it to me when I was really little,"
she says. Likewise, the major souvenir Candice
carted home from London has pride of place
– a small collection of old-school records she
effectively smuggled through customs. "I got
to Heathrow and they told me I was seven
kilos over weight. So I made my friend hold
my things while I got weighed again, then just
put it all back in," she says. "Although I did
throw away all my underwear because I thought,
I could buy new underwear in Australia but
I couldn't get these records there."

We're not home-renovating people. I like old stuff and everything, but I don't really know how to fix things.

The records now live in the couple's lounge room, which is probably their favourite spot in the house. Sunlight spills through the windows during the day and, at night, they can look out over the lights of Hobart – the city centre is a quick 10-minute zip up the highway, yet their neighbourhood feels peaceful, with plenty of trees and birdlife and the Derwent River just a short walk away.

Candice is pretty chuffed with the lounge room's couches, too – modern versions of the exact one she'd admired in an antique shop window for months. One day she and Murray walked into a furniture shop and discovered "the weird puffy couch" she'd been telling him about. "We found out it's a brand called Tessa Furniture, an Australian furniture designer based in Melbourne. So we saved up for ages to buy them."

Loads of their other knick-knacks are op shop finds – and Murray is a bit of a Gumtree addict with a particular eye for mid-century gems – though Candice says they mainly aim to live by 19th-century English designer William Morris's philosophy: "Have nothing in your house that you do not know to be useful, or believe to be beautiful." It doesn't, however, always work out that way. An attempt to buy curtains for the study, for instance, didn't quite make the "useful" category, because it turns out they're only borderline functional. Luckily, they make up for it by being rather pretty. "I went to the op shop and found those curtains and thought they were perfect and would fit perfectly," says Candice. "And then I put them up and they did not fit perfectly.

But I like how you kind of still see outside because they're not so long."

Outside, the couple popped up a fence to keep Oslo from escaping, and green thumb Murray has already plotted out a relatively serious vegie patch (he's largely responsible for all the indoor plant life, too). Candice has high hopes for their garden's yield come summer, considering a similar effort Murray made when they lived further north went gangbusters. "We could make dinner without buying anything because there was so much, which was a very good feeling," she says.

Home growing organic food like that is a Tassie hallmark, Candice says, along with the island's infamous winter chill, though she insists the cold's not as bad as people make out. "Murray will wear a t-shirt outside in winter. I'm a cold person, but I still only need an undershirt, a jumper and then a coat. I think people talk it up a bit," she says. "I actually really enjoy the four seasons thing and all the changes that come with it, the different vegetables you get and the way everything looks really different."

While they're both still young and can't rule out a return home to the mainland sometime in the future, Candice says for now they're thoroughly enjoying the chance to lap up Tasmania's relaxed and friendly vibe. "We definitely feel at home here," she says. "We love being able to do whatever we want, fixing up the garden, planting things, having Oslo run around the yard, playing music. No dramas." •

Abbey Rich

lives in an apartment in Brunswick
West, Melbourne. She is an artist
& fashion designer.

WORDS SAMANTHA PRENDERGAST PHOTOGRAPHS OLGA BENNETT

When Abbey Rich was 16 years old, she hatched a plan to move from the family home in Frankston, on the edge of Melbourne, to the city's inner-northern suburbs. "I like Frankston, but I always felt like I was on the outside looking in," she says. As a budding artist, Abbey wanted to live on her own, but be surrounded by other creative people. Determined to make it happen, she worked full-time at a supermarket and "saved like crazy". At 19, she packed up her things and moved to a one-bedroom unit on a quiet side street in Brunswick West, the place she now calls home.

"The property wasn't listed anywhere," Abbey says. "I didn't exactly know what I was doing, so went to the real estate agent and asked what was available. When they showed me this place, I saw the big windows and the floorboards and thought, I would *love* to live here." It was a surprise then, that with no rental history, she got it. The apartment, which is in a little block of three, had the natural light and floorboards she was after – the only other thing she really wanted was somewhere to plant vegies. With the yard paved in concrete, there's no real garden or even a grassy patch, but Abbey makes do with a collection of potted herbs that are shaded by a next-door neighbour's lemon tree. Her neighbours often find her sitting in the yard, reading. "Everyone who lives here is lovely," Abbey says. "The people next door just moved out and, when they went, they left me a picnic mat so I wouldn't be sitting on cold concrete all the time."

Just inside Abbey's front door is an airy open-plan living room that leads to a galley kitchen. At one end of the space, a door opens into the bedroom and bathroom. When she first moved into the unit, it doubled as her studio for her self-titled fashion label. "There were three big tables in the main room and sewing machines everywhere," she says. "It was very much a working domain and not so ideal for living." Now that Abbey keeps most of her work contained in her North Melbourne studio, her living space is much more relaxed. The walls are covered in artworks and knick-knacks, and the entire room is furnished with found, borrowed and inherited furniture.

The centrepiece is the compact pink and white sofa Abbey inherited from her parents. "My mum and dad have had the couch since they first moved out of home in their 20s," she says. "It's been a part of every house they've lived in." When Abbey was a kid, the couch belonged in her bedroom, so it's covered in childhood stains and memories. Everything else seems to complement the faded two-seater. In front of it, there's a pale, low-lying coffee table to hold magazines, a milk-crate bookshelf to store Abbey's collection of art books, a wooden set of pigeonholes full of art supplies, the odd pink chair and plenty of other pink bits and bobs. Works-in-progress are stacked against a ceiling-height easel that Abbey found on the side of the road. Finding roadside gems is a Rich family habit. "In Frankston, the hard rubbish is really good, so we always had new furniture but we never paid for it." One of her dad's finds is a speckled Laminex table that Abbey snaffled up for her space. "When he first brought it home I just thought it was completely ugly," she says. But six months later, it caught her eye. "I asked if I could take it with me and my dad pointed out that I hated the thing. But I really love it now."

Despite her hawkish eye for good hard rubbish, Abbey rarely adds new furniture to her home. Instead she tends to shift things around. "When I was growing up, I'd constantly rearrange my room and it would drive my parents mad. But this is on a whole new level." In a compact apartment, it's a way to change how she feels about the space. "Recently, I pushed my bed up against the window and it feels so luxurious to wake up and look outside." In her work as a fashion designer, Abbey tends to think in seasons.

Left page: Although Abbey now works mainly away from home, she keeps art supplies handy.

Above: Abbey likes to shift
things around; having
the bed by the window is
a recent thing and feels
quite luxurious, she says.

"When you finish creating something, you often want to move on and work on something new," she says. "In fashion, you can do a collection and be done with it." She applies the same logic to her artworks, which is why you won't see a whole lot of Abbey Rich originals on her walls. A few of her prints are dotted about the space, but otherwise her home is a revolving door of ideas and influences.

The one thing that doesn't change is the wall of artworks hung above the table near the front door. She likes to keep herself surrounded by works that remind her of friends. There's a portrait of Abbey and a friend, painted by her mum, a series of illustrations and small paintings, and a framed copy of the Guerrilla Girls' *The Advantages of Being a Woman Artist*. Most of the pieces are trades, something she started doing when she moved to Melbourne. Abbey's first swap was an illustration of a beanie-clad girl. "I was in a clothing store and an artist I really liked, Jacqui Burnes, was working there. We got chatting and she saw that I was knitting beanies, so she swapped a beanie for an illustration. Now I'm submitting work at her gallery and it's all very fun."

If the place has a downside, it's the size of the galley kitchen. "If it's clean, it's fine, but as soon as you put your shopping on the bench, it gets out of hand." Abbey likes to cook but the space limits her to a lot of one-pot meals. In a small space, with a tiny kitchen, entertaining can be difficult, but Abbey and her friends have worked out a bit of a system. "Because a lot of us live in this area, we sometimes just share food and go to each other's houses." It's also a nice way to replicate the vibe of a share house. Though Abbey planned to live alone, she's not averse to the idea of cohabitation. "Now that I don't have my work space in my home, I'd actually love to live with people," she says. "But I do also know that I'm very controlling in my aesthetic. Being inside my place is a bit like being inside my mind."

In today's Australia, it seems unusual to move straight out of home into a one-person unit, but Abbey is making it work. "I've been here for two years now, and it's hard to imagine leaving," she says. "But I've also come to a point where the house kind of works, it's finished, so I can feel this desire to get up and move and start again." •

Danni Harris & Alec Hall

live in Kensington, Adelaide, with
their dog, Muddy Waters. Danni studies
& works in volunteer organisations; Alec
is an artist who studies & works in
disability support services.

WORDS ASHLEIGH STEEL PHOTOGRAPHS BRI HAMMOND

Setting up camp in old houses, complete with decades of history and grime embedded in their walls, can be both charming and kind of annoying. "It's definitely got its quirks," says Danni Harris of the home she's shared for the past two years with her husband-to-be, Alec Hall. "Nothing ever works how it's supposed to, it's freezing in winter and the whole place creaks."

Not that any of that matters – they love the place. With the two of them working all sorts of odd hours in demanding jobs and studying on top of that, it's important that their home feels like a sanctuary from the world. "Alec does a couple of overnight shifts working with kids – it's nice to come home and wind down after that," says Danni.

They live in part of the heritage-listed Rising Sun Inn, which was established in the 1840s. Danni and Alec's digs, an expansive yet cosy two-storey, three-bedroom place, was one of three shops attached to the side of the hotel. Nearby, on a route Danni and Alec regularly take with their labrador Muddy Waters, are rows of old buildings with their original shopfronts. "I can just imagine the horse-drawn carts rolling down the street," says Alec. Historical plaques in the area date these buildings back to the early 1800s, so it's no wonder Danni and Alec feel the weight of history in their home. "The publican actually hung himself in our building," says Danni. "If you walk out onto the landing on the second floor you can see where it happened." Not that they dwell on such a morbid thing. "I haven't felt any eerie vibes in this house," says Alec, adding that he has in some of their neighbours' places.

The Rising Sun has been through plenty of renovations over the years. The property was divided into small apartments in the late '70s before being pieced back together into one building a couple of decades later. "It gets confusing when it comes to disputing gas bills because the lines have been converted backwards and forwards so many times," says Alec. Not to mention the funny external laundry and odd set-up with the electricity. There's also a particularly obtrusive fire escape, which blocks off a chunk of potential garden. "I'd like to make it more of a yard rather than a courtyard," he says. But the couple insists that it's the odd bits that add charm. "It's fun to work around the quirks rather than change anything," says Alec.

Left page: When Danni and Alec moved to Adelaide, they ditched most of their belongings and started again from scratch, working their way through South Australian junk shops.

Danni and Alec are in the unique and potentially intimidating situation of living next door to their landlords. But, says Alec, "They're very lovely so there's no problem there." And they also give the couple discounted rent to use the third bedroom as a storage space. "It just means every now and then they pop over to grab stuff," he says. Before the pair moved in, the property was mainly used for storage ("It was full to the brim with musical instruments and skis," says Alec), apart from the odd times when it was occupied by various family members of the landlords. At the initial inspection, Danni and Alec were amused to find a window had been left open for pigeons to set up camp in their potential pad. "It was kind of like that first scene in *Ghost* when they move into the house – a big open space and lots of sheets covering things," says Alec. Luckily, the rundown property was cleaned up before they moved in. "It just feels like a really nice space to be in," says Danni. "We were really happy when we got to secure it."

The front room, Danni and Alec's favourite and one they rearrange regularly, has a large bay window that serves as a reminder of the property's past life as a shop. "Sometimes the room's a designated workspace, and then it becomes a great place to host a big dinner party," says Danni. Adds Alec: "I like the idea that because it's such a big space we can change it all the time like a shop. I get bored quickly with how things look." Luckily, the fixed features of the house have also proved to be very useful, with a working fireplace downstairs making the chilly Adelaide winters more bearable. "Everyone goes crazy for the spiral staircase, too," says Alec, who points it out as another favourite feature.

When Danni and Alec made the move to Adelaide from Melbourne, they carted over all their collected bits and bobs, which turned out to be a rather futile task. "We ended up getting rid of most of it and started looking for new pieces," says Danni. Fortunately, adds Alec, "We have similar taste, so we haven't disagreed on a lot when it comes to how the place looks."

Scouring the South Australian junk shops is slightly different from op shopping in Melbourne. "You've got to go further out in Adelaide, but I think there are a lot of untapped resources," says Danni. On their first expeditions, the duo struck gold with a chesterfield couch and managed to snag two vintage leather theatre chairs from a closing cinema in town. "You've got to know where to look," says Alec. "And I think we've done a pretty good job of that." On the artwork front, with Alec being an artist, most pieces have been created by him or other creative friends.

It's not only the front room that gets shifted around from time to time. "We're in the process of converting the spare room upstairs into a workspace and setting up the sewing machines again," says Danni. They have so much room in their place, she says, that they're constantly trying to work out how to use it all. "I feel like if we're not utilising it we're wasting it." While the expansive space can be a luxury, it also comes with its cons: more space equals more places to pile up the mess. "It's a really large place to vacuum, particularly with our moulting dog," she says. "He's also the perfect height to knock things off tables."

As happy as they are in their perfectly imperfect, oversized place, it may not be home forever. "I think eventually we'd like to join the rest of the gang and buy our own place," says Alec, who relishes the idea of having full control over a space, in the way only an owner can. "That's the dream one day, but we're not in a huge rush for that." •

Eileen Braybrook & Stefan Delatovic
live in Brunswick, Melbourne,
with their cat, Mo. Eileen is a
textile designer & artist; Stefan
is a communications manager.

WORDS KOREN HELBIG PHOTOGRAPHS HILARY WALKER

Country kids Eileen Braybrook and Stefan Delatovic's big move to the city quite literally started with a bang. A week after driving the 840 kilometres south from Broken Hill to Melbourne, they awoke to a thunderous crash that shook their entire apartment. Turns out a car had ploughed through a bus stop into their front door, then fled the scene. "The front door is the only way in and it was completely jammed," Eileen says. "The fire department had to come and axe the door down so we could get out." Adds Stefan: "We were like, 'Everyone said the city was really hardcore and it's true!'"

Jokes aside, the couple actually was pretty nervy about the switch to city living. They both grew up in Broken Hill, a mining town where everyone knows everyone. "We'd never even filled out a rental application before. In Broken Hill, it was always just your mum's friend or something," Stefan says. They met as teens manning Woolies checkouts – Stefan would pass Eileen little jokes scrawled across the back of receipts, proving his wittiness without the need for terrifying real-life chat – and moved in together not long after. Eventually, they bought a big old house of their own and their future in Broken Hill seemed pretty set – until Eileen decided she wanted to study textile design in Melbourne.

"We settled on Brunswick because we were really scared of not being able to find our way around. I'd never even been on a tram before," Eileen says. "When I worked out where my uni campus was, we picked something really close, within two blocks of everything." They adopted a military-precision approach to house hunting and, incredibly for Melbourne, managed to land a rental almost immediately.

Things continued to fall into place when Stefan was offered a job as a community news editor. "When I took it, they said, 'Are you going to be OK commuting from Brunswick to Dandenong every day?' And I was like, 'Yeah, no worries,' because I didn't know where either of those places were," he says. That made for a hectic first few years, with Stefan leaving for work before daylight and returning home after dusk, while Eileen ran herself ragged studying

knitting and textile design at RMIT University. "I didn't have time for grocery shopping or cooking or even showering some days. It was really terrible," Eileen says. "But the outcome is that Stef is now an amazing cook."

Moving required a major downsizing effort, because their city pad is teeny, just two small bedrooms plus a tiny adjoined kitchen-living room. "We got a friend to measure up all the tight spaces and decided we could bring the washing machine and a couple of shelves and that was about it," Eileen says. It all had to happen at lightning speed, too, because Eileen's uni acceptance came through just six weeks before the semester started.

They ended up selling their big house and most of the stuff in it, though a few Broken Hill relics did make it to Melbourne, like the '60s sideboard their TV is plonked on. And, of course, their 14-year-old cat. "Mo's a secret cat, so I hope our landlord and real estate agent never read this," Eileen says. "She's like our child, so bringing her was non-negotiable." Mo was in the bad books for a while, though, after systematically shredding the enormous speakers for the Onkyo record player Eileen's dad picked up in the '70s.

Their Brunswick apartment was brand new when Eileen and Stefan arrived in 2011, basically just an empty white box. Having always lived in old houses, they weren't sure how they'd fit into such a sterile new place. But it ended up being a blessing of sorts for Eileen, who went nuts with the wildly colourful style she loves so much. "I actually get a bit self-conscious sometimes, that maybe it looks like a clown lives here. I do think it works, but every now and then I go, 'Oh my god, am I insane?'" she says. "Even when I was little, Dad used to take me to the tip to scavenge for bits of furniture and stuff, so maybe that's how I developed my eye, if you can call it that."

A few things made by Eileen, who's now a textile designer and lectures on knitwear, are hanging about, including a rug she made from recycled t-shirts. "Stef sacrificed a couple of t-shirts that probably didn't need to be shredded just yet," she admits.

Above: Some of the plants are ones the couple brought down from their old house in Broken Hill.

Eileen's also responsible for the enormous quantity of plants and even brought some down from Broken Hill, possibly accidentally breaking Victoria's plant quarantine rules.

Most of the artworks that bring splashes of colour to the walls were made by friends, but perhaps the most meaningful piece has pride of place on top of their dunny: a neat cross-stitch by Stefan's former editor Erin Lewis-Fitzgerald, featuring a squirrel with one nut and the words 'Fuck Cancer'. It's a reference to Stefan's brush with testicular cancer in 2014. "I had a really good run," Stefan says of the ordeal. "I found a lump, my GP checked it out, sent me for a test and then got me into the Peter MacCallum Cancer Centre really quickly. I just woke up with slightly less bits."

Thankfully, it was all over within a couple of months, yet both Eileen and Stefan were pretty shaken. After receiving the diagnosis, they both went straight home and joined a gym. "It sounds so silly. I can't believe we did that, as if it would make a difference," says Eileen. Adds Stefan: "Like, we're going to be healthy now!" Still, for Stefan, it worked in a way – he ended up losing more than 25 kilograms. "I'm just such a narrative story nerd," says Stefan, who now manages communications for Victoria's State Emergency Service. "I got wound up in the idea that the dinner party story had to be: 'Stefan got cancer and that's how he kicked off being a healthy guy.'" Eileen later made Stefan a little protective talisman of sorts, a nest made from peach tree cuttings – peach is a Chinese symbol of immortality and a healthy life – that hangs above their bed.

Eileen and Stefan still toy with the idea of moving to a bigger place, something spacious enough to have more than three people over for dinner at once, or with enough room for a comfy three-seater napping couch like the one they used to have in Broken Hill. "I think that's what we miss the most; we don't have a nice place to nap," says Eileen. "We do nap on the rug, but it's just not the same." Still, they like the "free theatre" of living across the road from a pub, even if it's a bit noisy on weekends, and the convenience of having Brunswick's tremendous eateries just a short walk away.

Plus, they've scored a little more space since Eileen moved her work into a Tinning Street studio, which made Stefan pretty happy because "there's no longer needles in all the couches". Says Eileen: "We've made our own little oasis. It's small, but for two people and a cat, it's very comfy. Just perfect." •

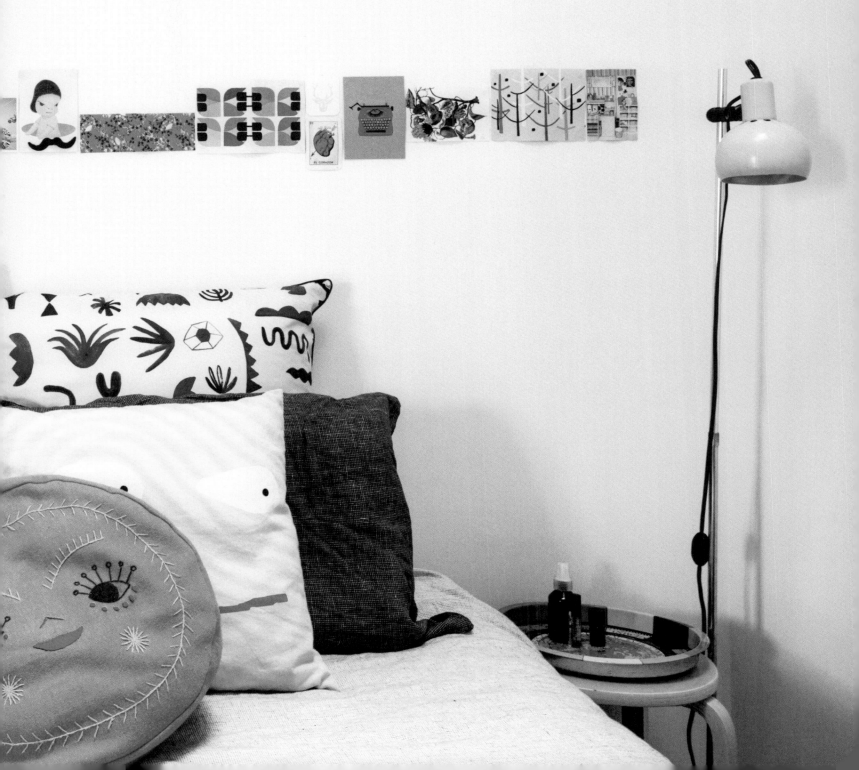

NEIGHBOURS IN FIVE HOUSES

IN CAMPERDOWN, SYDNEY, GET ON
LIKE A HOUSE ON FIRE.

INTERVIEWS ASHLEIGH STEEL **PHOTOGRAPHS** SASKIA WILSON

The residents of a street in Sydney's Camperdown are proof that the city can still offer that small town vibe, where neighbours rely on each other for much more than a cup of sugar. Eight years ago, Tess and Heath were the first of this gang to move into the street, getting buddy-buddy with their landlord Barry so they could recommend potential tenants whenever another house became available. The result is a community of various housemate combinations, ages, professions and dogs, with a common interest of creating not just a home, but a neighbourhood.

NUMBER 53 //
CASSIE STEEL
WRITER

Tess never thought I would agree to being next-door neighbours. Although the potential intensity of two good friends living side by side did cross my mind, my partner Majid and I really needed to get out of the tiny studio apartment we were living in. Tess convinced Barry that we were the perfect fit for the street, and after a quick look at the house, Majid and I only had a 10-minute deliberation in the park, while Barry waited across the road, to decide if we wanted to call it our new home. Luckily we agreed, and fell in love with the place, so much so that we're going to get married here in this very park. The aisle will quite literally be the crossing of the road from our front porch.

On a typical Saturday morning in the street, Majid and I will leave the house and have a quick chat to Heath, who is probably on the step next door with a cup of tea and a Scotch Finger, with Olive lying at his feet and Tess tinkering away in the kitchen. Then we'll pass Gary sitting out the front of his place with the paper and his dog Bill, and give a wave, moving on to see Phoebe, Camille and Adam pottering

around their house. We'll give their dog Teddy a pat and move onto the next house where Elliot will emerge after a wild night, telling us a crazy story about what he got up to. Majid will generally say, "Beers tonight?" and everyone will say, "Yep!"

MAJID DUBLOO
RETAIL MANAGER

I loved this house straightaway, mainly because it had a front and back yard. Our previous place had no dividing walls, making video game playing at night impossible without complaints from a sleepy Cass.

A lot of us moved into this street around the same time, creating this collective vibe of excitement to live in a neighbourhood like this. Our annual New Year's Eve parties have expanded over the years as more people are moving into the area. We'll put chairs on the street, fire up the barbecue and Heath ("DJ Scotch Finger") will crank out the tunes.

It's not just the street, I actually really like this house. It's the perfect size and we've put so much effort into the garden. We're never bored here because we know all the neighbours and we're so close to Newtown, where the action is. It's the best place I've lived in my whole life.

NUMBER 55 //
HEATH MANION
GRAPHIC DESIGNER

Saturday mornings are my favourite part of the week, sitting out on the front step with a tea, chatting to Majid and Cass and watching the neighbourhood go by. It reminds me of being home in Tasmania – everyone actually says hello to each other and seems willing to be part of a community. It's the nature of the cul-de-sac and having the park across the road – the social dynamic of this neighbourhood has evolved nicely.

Left page: Cassie and Majid and their place. They have the best backyard on the block.

Tess has been very proactive about encouraging our friends to move into the street. Whenever word got out that some tenants were vacating, Tess would be straight on the phone to our landlord: "Barry I've got someone! Can they move in?"

Summertime really brings everyone together out on the street. It started very organically; you walk out of your house on a warm evening and someone's out there having a drink, so you join in, too, and then someone else comes along. Then Majid started having birthday parties, and the New Year's Eve events developed.

Things are changing really quickly around here, with apartments and cafés going up everywhere. Now Barry has passed away, there's speculation that the family will sell all these terraces to developers, which would be a real shame. I can see the dynamic of the street winding down – Cass and Majid are getting married soon, people are moving out, things are evolving. I think you get some good years here and then it's time to move on.

TESS FLINT-ÖZMERT
FLORIST, STUDENT AND NANNY

It often feels like little Europa out here, with people hanging things from the top balcony of the terraces, all in a line and having a chat. When I stand up here, I feel like I'm in a treehouse with that beautiful big tree just outside our bedroom. If that tree goes, I'll go with it – I would chain myself to it.

Gary was the first person I persuaded Barry to rent one of these places to. I met Gary while I was working at a café up the road – the kind where you chat to locals for hours. He was recently widowed and needed a place to move to with Bill, his dog. Next up were Cass and Majid, who I thought wouldn't want to live here, but I was pleasantly surprised. Our place is the mirror image of their place next door – we're very close to each other but there's a wall that allows everyone to retreat to their own space. Cass and I have been friends since high school, but being neighbours has really brought us together to be almost like a little family. It's the best thing that's happened here on this street.

Left page, top: Tess and Heath with Olive, and inside their house. Below: Gary with Bill, and shelves in his living room. This page, above: Tess and Heath's place.

Travelling has always been a part of my life so I like to display my collected worldly trinkets around the home. Although Heath often whinges about the overload of "old stuff", I'm very attracted to second-hand furniture with character and a story. I think, "Do what you want to do" with your house; it would be boring if they were all the same.

NUMBER 57 //
GARY STOCKS
ADMIN ASSISTANT

I tend to live a lot of my life on the front porch because there's the availability of more interactions with people. I think this comes from being solo for long periods of time – I've always kept my communication with community by sitting out the front, reading the newspaper with a cup of tea.

I rented an apartment around the corner for 20 years before my two-year-old border collie Bill and I got the boot five years ago. Tess suggested I move into the house next door to her that had just come up for rent. Barry was happy to take recommendations for tenants so he didn't have to go around hunting or putting it out to an agent. If he thought you were an all right person, that was it.

This row of small terraces was built for workers at the Fowler potteries down the road, which produced utilitarian ceramic wares such as toilets and sewerage pipes. While the properties now seem to be perfect for one or two people, originally families with six or seven children were sharing them. They are astonishingly narrow – you couldn't swing a cat in them. The frontage of the street is heritage listed, as it is one of the few places in the area with all the lines of roofs still joined together. It's important to keep that piece of Sydney history.

I love being sandwiched among the younger people. Despite the age gap we enjoy relating to each other – it's good to see them all growing up, and of course I can chat to their mothers.

NUMBER 61 //
PHOEBE HOGAN
INTERIOR ARCHITECT

Camille, my sister, Adam, my partner, and I have been living together for the past few years in various places like one little family unit. We are completely comfortable and have no problem walking around in our underwear or yelling at each other for leaving shoes in the hallway. Living with a sister you get a bonus extra wardrobe, which is great, except perhaps when the tables turn and your things go missing.

As an interior designer and creative person in general, I tend to collect a lot of stuff. I'm always having to hide away my books and knick-knacks so they don't look messy for Camille, who prefers a minimalist aesthetic. Styling this place has been an interesting lesson in compromise for all three of us.

Adam and I had been coming to Tess's parties for years, so we knew the potential of our future home when we moved in. We all live in these little mirror-image terraces, but there's nothing cookie cutter about them – we can appreciate the individual quirks in each place. I'll walk into Tess's house and admire her purple floor or envy Cass and Majid's kitchen; and they wish they had our larger laundry. In terms of decorating, everyone's homes are an expression of their personalities.

In summer I find myself out the front doing some gardening and swapping seedlings with neighbours. No one I know has this kind of neighbourhood; it would feel really hard to leave this.

CAMILLE HOGAN
ACCOUNT MANAGER

Some of my colleagues have a good laugh and say I live on Ramsay Street. Funnily enough, I even got a job out of living here – Heath works at a creative agency and put me forward for an account manager position. We've been both workmates and neighbours for almost two years.

Phoebe calls her colourful and eclectic style "organised chaos"; I'm much more of a black and white person, but because we're sisters we can fight out our decorating differences in the open. For years I've lived in share houses with some interesting characters, so I can appreciate the comfort factor of nesting with family – none of those passive-aggressive housemate moments. Besides, I like to joke that I'm Adam and Phoebe's practice child.

It's hard to imagine looking at other properties in Sydney; we really are in such a good spot here with a huge park across the road, three cafés within 40 metres of our front door and friends all along the street. You just wouldn't get that anywhere else.

ADAM STONE
VISUAL DESIGNER

I think this house has set an incredibly high benchmark for what constitutes a happy home. What can I say? I'm in love with Phoebe, and Cammy is the sister I never had – it's a perfect dynamic for a household. We moved in here two years ago from an apartment in Kirribilli that didn't quite have the room for a fourth housemate – Cammy's kelpie, Teddy.

Tess is an old friend of ours and always keeps her finger on the pulse of the goss on the street, so suggested to Barry that the four of us would be perfect tenants for a soon-to-be vacant property on the street. While we did have to give up views of Sydney Harbour, we couldn't ask for a better bunch of neighbours. There are hangs in the park, epic costume parties and plenty of spontaneous Sunday night get-togethers that tend to make Monday a little difficult. Some of my mates don't understand the concept of hanging out with neighbours, but they just don't know what they're missing out on.

The house itself is small, but we manage to make room for board game nights, Phoebe's art projects and my tinkering with tech and bicycles.

We lost poor Barry, our landlord, last year, so we'll have to wait and see how long we'll be able to stay here. I just hope we never lose this.

NUMBER 63 //
ELLIOT BERRYMAN,
CHEMICAL ENGINEER

I moved into the street a year ago when I was relocating from Newcastle to Sydney for work. I used to play in a band with my now flatmate Blake, who said he had a room going in an old terrace house in Camperdown with his dog Neddy Boy. I love the style of the Sydney terrace, and tend to use our shared home space as a place to relax and play music. There's always a few instruments kicking around in our front room for impromptu jam sessions.

It's great hanging out with friendly neighbours, especially being relatively new to Sydney. There's always something social going on around here – whether it's drinks in the park across the road or *Game of Thrones* nights at Cass and Majid's.

I like that all our houses don't feel like rentals. Each resident has been able to make their own space into something that really reflects their personalities. •

Left page, above: Elliot and his place. Below, from left, Heath, Adam, Phoebe, Tess, Cassie, Camille, Gary, Majid and Elliot, with Teddy and Bill.

Hayley & Chadd Kessner
live in Catterick, WA, with
their three children & great
Dane. Hayley is a maker of
images, stories & art; Chadd
is a builder & carpenter.

WORDS ASHLEIGH STEEL PHOTOGRAPHS RACHEL WOODS

Hayley and Chadd Kessner have always tried to instil in their children the idea that home isn't bound to four walls – it's wherever you are with the people you love. "We have a bit of a loose motto in our house, that change is good for the soul," says Hayley. But after nearly a decade spent as a FIFO (fly in, fly out) family due to Chadd's work in the mines, Jaspa, 12, Sascha, 11, Scarlett, 5, and Behemoth Aristotle the great Dane, are enjoying putting down some roots on 25 acres of Australian bush in the tiny town of Catterick, Western Australia.

After a tip-off from her sister, who discovered the neighbouring community of Bridgetown while at a music festival, Hayley, on the hunt for a proper home, and Chadd, keen to try out his new Harley Fat Boy, took a ride down south from Perth to scope the place out. "As soon as we rode down the main street, we knew there was something special about this place," says Hayley. "We started looking in the real estate windows straightaway."

After tossing up between two properties, the couple settled on a spacious, two-storey farmhouse at the end of a winding gum-lined driveway. The previous owners had taken eight years to build the property by hand, selecting each wall stone piece by piece from the local quarry, and reclaiming jarrah from the old railway. With a strong repurposing ethos, the husband and wife duo used no new material to construct the house, with each window and door found at the local salvage yard or from friends' farms. After 33 years, the pair passed on the property to Hayley and her family, who appreciate this handmade history. "Everywhere you look you find another little detail you hadn't noticed," says Hayley. "Every part is a little bit quirky, a little bit wonky, but it all seems to fit together just fine."

Despite the charm of imperfection, there were a number of renovations Hayley and Chadd had to address before they could relocate their whole gang of tween-agers and pets just a few months ago. That included ripping

out carpets, installing ceiling fans, replacing light fittings, adding windows, replacing the hot water system and toilet – a team effort from carpenter and builder Chadd and former interior designer turned general creative Hayley. "Although I no longer work as an interior designer, it has been super important in how I design my home," she says. "I know all the rules so I can break them."

Spaces have been set up to encourage specific usage: a designated music living room with instruments, a record player and vinyl on display fosters a family appreciation for music. "Working out what space you want to use for what activity helps the kids settle in really quickly," says Hayley. The pair designed their home with a focus on how the whole family would use it – relaxing and reconnecting after a long nomadic stint. "Everything is cosy and comfy and not precious," says Hayley, who sought to steer clear of creating a contrived space with everything in its right place. "I really despise 'same-same' homes where you know exactly where they got every piece of furniture and every piece of art hanging on the wall," she says. "I like to make everything myself, and it's only when I can't that I'll go searching for it somewhere else." After finding an Australian poetry book at the local farmers' market, Hayley ripped out the pages and created a collaged wall of words. "I have a big love for poetry – it's lovely to stop and have a little read whenever you walk past," says Hayley, "It makes for great conversation, too."

Relocating to a family home three times the size of their previous dwelling proved both a liberating and challenging experience. They brought all the furniture they could with them, but needed to source a lot of extras from Gumtree and op shops to fill the vast space. An open-plan kitchen, dining room and living area is beneath a mezzanine level of parents' living space complete with a master bedroom and wraparound balcony. Downstairs, off the living room, is an opening that leads to the designated games room where Hayley and Chadd encourage their kids to make craft.

Above: One wall in the house has been papered with pages Hayley tore from a poetry book she picked up at a local farmers' market.

Admittedly, the kids are still trying to get their heads around the idea that their new home is almost entirely 'screen free' and that they're now living in the middle of the bush, where friends are more than a short bike ride away. "Surprisingly, they took to it pretty quickly," says Hayley of the iPad-free life. "Most days they're off building teepees in the bush, making BMX tracks with their dad or collecting firewood on the old ride-on lawnmower." Inside, too, the novelty of this unique home is not lost on the kids: "They find it pretty amusing that we have our very own 'rock walls' that they can climb without having to go anywhere," says Hayley.

The home is surrounded by a mixture of natural bushland and plantation blue gums, with only an acre or two clear for the house and orchard. Chook pens are dotted across the yard and the original ramshackle shed that the previous family lived in during their eight-year build still stands strong.

Hayley is the first to admit that having a handy husband has eased the renovation burden. Chadd picks up part-time gigs as a carpenter while turning his building skills to the home. "We've made things for each space in the house," says Hayley. "Having a chippy as a husband is always a good thing." While the pair have improvements planned

for the property, including a complete kitchen overhaul, the house feels comfortable enough for the family to put up their feet. "We're pretty much at a point where we can happily chill out on the weekend and not feel like there's a million reno jobs that need to be done ASAP." Hayley works from home on her various art and styling projects, without a designated space, instead preferring to move from room to room with the changing light. On the future to-do list is setting up the old shed as a studio workspace, where she will install potter's wheels, a kiln, a long table and some comfy couches to make the space her own.

While it's still early days for Hayley, Chadd and their gang, this house is really beginning to feel like a home. With renovations and extensions planned, and the need for a settled space while the boys get through high school, it seems like this Australian bush haven will be a place for the group to put down their bags for a while.

As for what the long-term future holds: "We never say forever – that's kind of our catch-cry," says Hayley, who wants the family to remain open to whatever adventures may present themselves. "Although we do love it here, if Italy called tomorrow and asked if we wanted to go hang out there for a while, we most definitely wouldn't say no." •

Emma Byrnes & Pete Barrett
live with their kids, Arkie, Ziggy
& Alby, in Fitzroy North, Melbourne.
Emma is a designer, photographer
& innovator; Pete is a journalist
& copywriter.

WORDS MIA TIMPANO PHOTOGRAPHS HILARY WALKER

Bikkies. Free ones. That's what sold Emma Byrnes and her husband, Pete Barrett, on a house just near Melbourne's Merri Creek. "They were giving them out at the inspection," she says, "and we immediately thought, 'This place is so cosy and loving and just real.'" Of course, it wasn't just the yummy treats that inspired the couple to turn up on auction day. There was also the fact that the house was located in Fitzroy North. "Pete's a real urbanite, while I could live in the country or the seaside," Emma says. "This felt like a really good compromise, because it's tucked away among all the gumtrees and the creek is right behind us. So this has been our little urban oasis where we get access to all the good stuff."

The house wasn't in perfect nick when they arrived. Far from it, in fact. "It was all brown wallpapers, brown carpets and big air conditioning units stuck in windows, so the light wasn't really getting in," Emma says. Since renovations weren't in the couple's plans, home improvements happened haphazardly. "We gave some rooms a lick of paint and pulled up the doggy hair carpet," she says. "There was carpet in the kitchen; stuff like that just doesn't work." Sanding back the floorboards wasn't an option either. The bloke they asked to do the work refused on the grounds they were too thin – shaving off the top would mean they might fall through. So instead, Emma and Pete slapped some paint on them. Green. A random choice of Emma's. "I haven't thought anything through in terms of interiors," she says, laughing. "Green's my favourite colour, and I don't wear green, because it looks funny on my skin, so I guess it's a good way of having it in my life. It also felt like it matched with the trees outside."

Some items in the house are still original, though, like the laminate kitchen table, which matches the kitchen benchtops. "It's nifty match-match," Emma says.

"Not much matches around here, so that's interesting." The table isn't just a visual highlight. It's also one of a collective of spaces from which Emma runs Heartland, her creative agency; the others are a small studio in the Nicholas Building in the centre of Melbourne, and the spaces of the small businesses with whom she collaborates. With a professional background in photography, interactive web design and small business management, Emma is ideally suited to helping folks "visually articulate what they're doing". The work is also ideally suited to her family life.

"Having three children is very much an all-consuming situation," she says. "So I thought, maybe I'll just combine everything I've ever known and loved into one thing and call it a bespoke creative agency and see what happens." Her clients include local folk making textiles, sustainable furniture and a variety of other things with their hands. "I'm just totally attracted to people who are doing their own thing, to the beat of their own drum," Emma says. It may have something to do with how she was raised, helping out at her mum's European-style coffee house in Sydney; little Emma did all the business's signage.

These days, Emma is keen to foster her own kids' creativity. Laundry drawers are stuffed with craft supplies, and all the ornaments around the place double as toys. With an original Dawn Tan illustration hanging on the kitchen wall and a collection of crystals bestowed on the family by Emma's sister in the living area, you might think a 'mitts off' policy would reign in Casa Byrnes-Barrett. After all, what if something got ruined? "If it gets ruined, it gets ruined," Emma says. "All these things become part of the kids' fantasy land. And they set up some amazing things." Plus, in Emma's view, nothing they own is too precious. "I don't want to be walking around saying, 'Don't touch that!' I want us all to be comfortable in this space."

Left page: Quite by chance, the kitchen table matches the benchtops. Emma's favourite colour, green, is used throughout the house.

The kids sleep wherever they please. "We're a co-sleeping family," Emma says. Their son, Ziggy, aged eight, has taken to sleeping on the lounge room shag pile rug, while son Alby, aged three, is starting to snooze less with his parents and is carving out his own space in the kids' communal bedroom (Emma sets up a mattress and makes a "cosy corner" for him at night). Daughter Arkie, who counts a quill among her favourite possessions, is another matter. At 12, she's on the cusp of teendom, and is eyeing off the spare bedroom, which up till now has offered Emma and Pete another space to get some shut-eye. "When we come back from our next road trip, we'll probably make that the official room for Arkie," Emma says, "but at the moment it's just a bit of neutral space."

The family loves travelling, and most recently visited Vietnam – not for a jaunt, but a three month-long haul. World-schooling the kids is Emma's fantasy, but Pete's less keen on the idea. "He thinks it's a bit out there," she says. "So this was, once again, a really good compromise." An added bonus was being able to stay in touch with clients back home, by virtue of the fact Vietnam is only three to four hours behind Melbourne timewise. Neighbours stayed in touch, too. One even asked if the family wouldn't mind picking up 200 dollars' worth of lanterns. "We were like, 'Yeah, sure,'" Emma says. True, the task led the clan on a "wild goose chase" through Hoi An, but they were glad of the chance to explore the lantern factory and meet the makers. They even helped install the lanterns, back here in Australia.

*Above left: The kids'
cubby house, made by
Pete, sits on top of the
chicken coop.*

←

"We're very engaged in the neighbourhood," Emma says. "Because there's no traffic in the street, kids just run in and out of each others' houses all day, every day. I can turn around and there'll be eight children in the house. It's just this evolving daily exchange of friends and family, almost like an unofficial commune." The front yard often plays host to kids' gatherings, a favourite spot being among the fruit trees. Thanks to their chickens redistributing seeds from the compost in the soil, there's practically a whole orchard of produce to enjoy: apples, peaches, nectarines, apricots, and about 500 limes every year. Friends pop past to take a batch of the citrusy yield off their hands, with very tall mate Dave getting the best stash of all, as he's able to reach the top.

Tucked around the back of the house is another kids' haven: a cubby house that sits on top of the chooks' roost, Pete's own handiwork. "This is actually a really cute spot to serve up morning tea," Emma says. "And it's cool, because you can stand up there and be a pirate." Tea-drinking and swashbuckling times aside, the family tends not to spend too much time out the back. Though Emma says: "If you were to renovate our place, this might

become a really amazing area." Whether they'd consider doing so is another matter. "I don't know," she says. "It's so frigging expensive to do anything! We have just started thinking we should come up with a plan for what we're doing, because soon we'll have much larger bodies in this little space." Pete did recently explore the under-house area, a storage space they considered excavating and turning into a den, but the discovery of asbestos rubble put the brakes on that one – at least for now.

In the meantime, Emma will continue working on Heartland down one end of the kitchen table (the end nearer the AC outlet; Emma's Mac power cord can only stretch so far), and the kids will continue playing dress-ups in the street and getting up to all manner of shenanigans. At a recent auction, the neighbourhood's small army of children turned up, resplendent in assorted old-fashioned garments, yelling at the top of their lungs. That night Arkie explained the kids' motives to Emma. "She said, 'We all just decided to yell and scream, so whoever buys the house will really have to like kids.' And the people who moved in love kids, so it worked." •

Kyra Bartley & David Collins
live with their cat, Pepper, in a
warehouse in St Peters, Sydney.
Kyra is an animator; David is
a photographer.

WORDS LETA KEENS PHOTOGRAPHS CARINE THEVENAU

CAT | POES | "POOS"
GOOD | GOED | "GOOT"
HI | HOI | "HOY"
Bye | DOEI | "DEWJ" (HOW-DO)
WELLDONE | GOED ZO | "GOOT ZOUGH"

Welcome

Angel was here 5/4/16

HORSE PAARD | DOG | HOND | "HONT"
EVERYBODY | IEDEREEN | "IEDREEN"
SUGAR | SUIKER | "SOIKER"
Sleepwell | Welterusten | Welturusten
peanutButter | pindakaas | pinn-DA-CASE

Left page, above: A couple
from Amsterdam, who
have stayed on for months
after renting part of the
place on Airbnb, try to
teach Kyra and David
a few Dutch words.

**Furniture gets handed on to friends.
Clothes and books and other things do
as well. It's not too often, though, that a
whole house gets passed around, but Kyra
Bartley and David Collins' place is such
a beauty that, for the past 15 years or so,
no one's wanted to let go of it completely.
"A friend of ours was living here, but when
he headed over to London, he tapped me on
the shoulder and told me the warehouse
was coming up," says animator Kyra Bartley.
She and David, a photographer, hadn't been
long back from working in Cambodia and
were looking to move out of their "crappy
little terrace house" into something more
interesting. "Before our friend lived here,
another friend had it," she says. "It's so
good, it definitely stays in the family."**

It will probably be a while before Kyra and
David pass it on to anyone else; she says
they want to "hang onto it as long as humanly
possible". One of the owners is part of a
boy band, "and they are in LA doing their
thing. We've got it until they come back."
She reckons they're the "best landlords you
could possibly ask for". When they first moved
in, Kyra and David asked if they could build a
cyc wall for David's photographic work; the
landlords immediately said yes, then emailed
a week later asking what a cyc wall was.

The two-storey warehouse is set up with
pretty well a whole apartment plus photo
studio and outside bathroom downstairs;
upstairs is more living space, bedroom,
open bathroom ("You have to be pretty
comfortable with your partner"), laundry
and David's office. From time to time,
especially when they go away, David and
Kyra rent out downstairs on Airbnb – recently,
one couple from Amsterdam, Sander van den
Hurk and Sacha Verbeek, decided to stay on.
"We didn't think we'd ever be able to have
housemates because there's no privacy, but
it feels like a nice communal environment,"
says Kyra. "It's like living in separate houses,
but we get to do things together."

In the same way that the warehouse, a former
switchboard factory, was handed on to them,
so, too, was some of the furniture. A great big

table sits in a corner of the downstairs room:
"That's been here for at least the last three
people," says Kyra. Apart from being far too
big for any normal living space, it's impossible
to move as one of its legs is broken. In the
upstairs area, a chandelier and an ornate
mirror in the bathroom are leftovers from
previous tenants. Photo shoots have also been
an unlikely source of homewares – the table
in the kitchen, for instance, stayed on after
a commercial. One company wanted to trade
several days of studio time for furniture, but
Kyra and David would have ended up with
truckloads of unwanted stuff – they turned
down that particular job.

They've bought the odd piece from friends,
including the giant sofa in the living area,
which is big enough to sleep on. "It's fun
because you can play with scale here
more than you usually can," says Kyra.
Average-sized furniture looks tiny in the
space. "We tried some Ikea bookshelves,
and they looked dwarfed," says David.

They've also picked up bits and bobs from
local junk shops – a little metal table and chair
set sits just by the window in the front hallway.
"The sun streams in there in the afternoon
– it's a really nice spot for a cup of tea," says
Kyra. She livened the set up with a coat of
paint – part of her plan, says David, to create
"a Mexican picnic theme" in the hallway.
The AstroTurf, too, continues the outdoor
look. "Dave wasn't such a fan at first, but
he's come around to it."

Even though Kyra loves living in the
warehouse, she's not so mad on the "standard
industrial-style vibe. When you're living in
a warehouse, you want to do something
different. I love colour and pattern and wanted
to make sure the space didn't take itself too
seriously." As well as the cheerful hallway
furniture, that colour and pattern comes
from things like the paintings by David's best
mate Jan Van Dijk and the glass shaded lamp
that Kyra nabbed from her dad, who lives in
Brisbane, when he was in clearout mode.
"He sent me photos of a whole bunch of stuff
and asked me if I wanted it," she says. "We got
a car specially in Brissy and drove it down."

The only concession to the industrial look is, as Kyra describes it, "the stupid Foba stand" that sits on the edge of David's studio. "When we first set up the studio, pretty much our first client wanted to book it for three weeks to do a cookbook. He was all booked to go when he asked us if we had a Foba. We didn't, so lost the job – we spent thousands of dollars to get one and nobody has used it since." At least it looks "quite studio-ey" says David.

The warehouse has been used as a location for shoots which, at first, was hard for David. "I'm a little bit controlling, not in a big way, but I just worry about stuff. The surprising – the shocking – thing is it all comes back immaculately, even the television connections are put back correctly." Adds Kyla: "Because of the nature of it, it's a pretty robust space – things can get moved around." It does have its problems, though – it leaks, it's freezing in winter and boiling hot in summer. "It's like camping indoors," says David.

Upstairs, Kyla and David's space is not quite so extreme on the temperature front. "At least there's some ventilation there," says Kyla. It's pretty noisy, though, as the trucks thunder along the road outside day and night. "Luckily we're both good sleepers, although the first couple of weeks we lived here, I had crazy

nightmares that a truck was about to run me over," says Kyra.

Afternoon is a particularly nice time of day upstairs, although those golden shafts of light do show how dusty the space is. David's the one who does most of the cleaning – "I work from home, so it gets to me first" – while the kitchen is Kyra's favourite spot. "I've never had that much kitchen space before – I love cooking and am pretty expansive about it. I like everyone to know I'm making lots of stuff."

For David, his favourite place is the outside bathroom. The only downside of having housemates, he says, is that he no longer gets to use it. "It probably doesn't look much, but it's pretty spectacular, especially when it's raining."

It's not just the warehouse they love; it's the whole neighbourhood, which David says is the closest thing he's found yet to his home suburb of West End, Brisbane. "It's my favourite place to live in Sydney," he says. "It's colourful and multicultural, and feels more local and real than some other areas we've lived in. In those other places, I felt like I was living in someone else's home." Adds Kyra: "It's more of a community here. We've found our little spot." •

Left page, above:
The Foba stand, bought
for one shoot, is near
the glass doorway.

Rachel Burke & Thomas Lynch
live with their sausage dogs, Daphne
& Daisy, in Stafford, Brisbane. Rachel
is a designer & stylist; Thomas is
a criminal lawyer.

WORDS KATE VELING PHOTOGRAPHS NATALIE MCCOMAS

When Rachel Burke and Thomas Lynch first inspected the house they now call home, they didn't see eye to eye. Thomas struggled to see past the dowdy furniture, crappy carpet and garish bedroom walls. Rachel fell hard for the '40s post-war cottage. It even had a dog door for their sausage dog, Daphne.

On the drive home, there followed what Thomas diplomatically describes as an "exchange" and Rachel freely admits was a tantrum. "I wigged out!" she said. "It was the last place we saw after inspecting a series of bleak-looking houses. As soon as I walked in, I knew it was the place for us. It had loads of character but didn't require a crazy amount of renovations like some of the other properties we had seen. It just felt right from the get-go."

They managed to reach a mutual agreement and have now been happily installed in their home for two years. "We previously lived in a very tiny apartment, so moving into this place has been so incredible," says Rachel. "It's amazing what a few extra rooms can do for you. The extra space also allowed us to get our second dog, Daisy, which was really the cherry on top."

With the help of Rachel's mum, who lives nearby, they undertook some minimal but very effective renovations, putting in a new bathroom, ripping up the gross carpet to reveal beautiful old floorboards and painting the walls in neutral tones (a nice change from the hot tamale red in the master bedroom).

As Rachel's a fashion designer, stylist, hardcore crafter and textile designer and Thomas is a criminal lawyer, it's hardly surprising that their view of the world isn't always the same. Rachel's design projects are generally vibrant and often sparkly. As she puts it, she loves to "bedazzle" things. Thomas is more understated, but the two have struck the perfect balance within their shared space.

"Because his approach is so minimal, I try to be respectful of that with my general decor," says Rachel. "We are conscious of not turning the whole house into a tinsel wonderland. I try to keep the crazier aspects of my aesthetic to my workroom. I can be pretty wacky and fruity, but I also love my quiet, relaxed moments, too. The house is balanced between spaces of lots of colour and texture, then more relaxed spaces like our dining and lounge room. The more chilled rooms in the house are definitely more reflective of Thomas. I love this balance, as we really use the different rooms for different purposes and feelings."

Most of their furniture comes from op shops, and all their trinkets and treasures are imbued with personal significance. There are souvenirs from their honeymoon in Japan, Rachel's collection of found paper cranes, as well as ceramics, paintings and ornaments she has made. "We want the house to be a reflection of who we are, and the adventures we have had together," she says.

Being homebodies, Rachel and Thomas love nothing more than sitting with their sausage dog daughters, drinking tea, listening to music and pottering around. Thomas' favourite spot is on the couch with his feet on the coffee table because, "our house, our rules!". Rachel's is the dining room. "We will often play board games in there and listen to music while eating snacks and just relaxing. It also gets amazing light during the day and is really just a great chill zone." They also gather there for a regular Thursday night dinner with Rachel's family.

Thomas initially had the idea to take off the door of the dining room to open up the house. Although it did let more light into the living area, it created problems when Daisy had trouble toilet training and decided the dining room was her favourite place to pee. Daphne also delighted in barking at possums on the back deck and people passing by. "We realised, one day, if we put the door back on all our problems would be solved," says Rachel. And they were.

If the calmer spaces are more reflective of Thomas, then Rachel's workroom is where her bedazzling side shines. Stepping through the door is a bit like getting a confetti bomb in the face. The room is a riot of colour, craft supplies, tinsel and pom-poms. Rachel works on craft projects and commissioned pieces, plans and prepares for freelance workshops, paints, sews and carries out all kinds of crafty, creative activities in here. It's all very neatly organised, with a place for everything and everything in its place.

"This house inspires so much of my personal creative work," she says. "Most of my ideas begin in my crafty studio and come to fruition throughout the house. I am always picking up tinsel and pom-pom offcuts from the floor because of this very thing. I do a lot of photo shoots here, too, and can always find something new in it to tell a story."

Rachel has recently made room for Thomas in her studio, which has now been dubbed The Craft and Draft Room (she crafts, he drafts legal documents). His desk is a corner of calm in a chaos of colour. "I had this room to myself but then we realised we weren't seeing each other for really large stretches of time, so we decided to merge," says Rachel. "It's made working in there even more fun. I can now tap him on the head with pipe cleaners if I need to show him something, which he just loves."

Rachel also has plans for underneath the house. Like many Queenslanders, there's a large area downstairs that mirrors the main house. They'd love to wall it in, spruce it up and convert it into more creative space. "It would make the most incredible studio," she says. "I am starting to explode a little bit out of our current workspace."

Thomas and Rachel are so happy in their humble home that they even enjoy cleaning it, although this love of domestic duties does not extend to laundry. "We are both contributors to an ongoing bath-drobe," says Rachel. "Meaning that we often just chuck our clothes into the bath until it reaches a critical, shameful mass. I do wish the laundry was not downstairs as often I forget it exists... and then forget that we should be doing laundry."

Apart from that minor detail, these two reckon their house is pretty much perfect. "It's such a relaxing, heavenly place to be," says Rachel. "This is a bit morbid, but the other day I asked Thomas where he would like his ashes sprinkled (because, you know, it's good to be clear on this shit), and he said the front yard. After crying hysterically I had to agree. The house just holds such happiness and good vibes for us. Oh gosh, it sounds like we are in love with our house, doesn't it!" •

I'M SORRY THAT
I WORRY ABOUT

I'M SORRY
I EVER MET

I'M SORRY THAT I KEEP SAVING
YOUR LIFE EVEN THOUGH YOU
WANT SO BADLY FOR IT TO END

I'M SORRY I STILL MISS
YOU AND THE FUR BABIES.

I'M SORRY WE DIDN'T
WORK OUT.

THESE APOMOGIES ARE...
EMOTIONALLY FRAGILE so
PLEASE DON'T TOUCH THEM
Thanks!

Steph Hughes & Mia Mala McDonald
live in Brunswick, Melbourne,
with their cat, Chookie. Steph is an
illustrator; Mia is a photographer.

WORDS SAMANTHA PRENDERGAST **PHOTOGRAPHS** MIA MALA MCDONALD **PORTRAIT** OLIVIA MROZ

In a quiet corner of Brunswick, Steph Hughes and Mia Mala McDonald are creating their first family home. When Steph moved in seven years ago, it was a share house for four. "I was in my mid-20s, looking for a place to live, and it was the cheapest, cheeriest house I could find," she says. "We were all old, old friends and there was a lot of revelry."

Over the years, friends of friends have moved in and out of the sprawling house, leaving behind typical share-house debris: miscellaneous tents, flotsam bits of mail, and the occasional mysterious wall stain. One by one, flatmates moved on and, a couple of years ago, Steph's partner, Mia, moved in. "At that point there was hardly anything here," Steph says. "We had gotten rid of the last of the clutter – rotting bike corpses and things like that – then we did a big paint, fixed things up, and turned it into our little home." The pair now share their space with their Burmese cat, Chookie. And, in a few months' time, they are expecting a baby.

"To me it feels like a classic old family home," Mia says of the three-bedroom house, with its '80s tacked-on lean-to at the back. At the front, bedrooms lead off a central hallway, one now used as Steph's studio, and another nabbed for the baby. "That used to be our walk-in wardrobe, but we're happy to compromise with the baby on something," says Mia, a photographer who also runs the artists' complex, Magic Johnston in Collingwood, a few suburbs away. Steph is much more of a homebody. "We call her the Mayor of Munro," Mia says, referring to the name of their street. "Steph sits at the front window and watches all of the neighbours from her desk." Steph denies her role as the neighbour watch-woman, but one summer day she did notice a fire coming from a neighbour's house and ended up being the first on site. "It was something like 45 degrees, and when I saw smoke I wondered why someone would be having

a barbecue." Moments later she was helping an old lady out of her burning home.

Their own house has always been special to Steph, who has spent years cultivating a thriving vegie patch and making memories with friends and housemates. But when it came time for Mia to consider moving in, she wasn't entirely convinced. She and a whole load of other people had just been kicked out of The Paterson Building, an old furniture store that had been home to artists since the '60s and was about to be turned into apartments (see SPACES 2). "At first I wasn't so sure that we could make this place work," she says. "It's got to be the cheapest house you can rent in Melbourne, and with that comes a lot of 'charm'." Some parts of that 'charm' were more confronting than others. Along with holes in the walls and carpet in the kitchen, there were lights that sparked when you turned them on, and an oven that was completely kaput. "But we figured that if we lived here for a year and tried to put a bit of effort into fixing the place up, it could work," Mia says. "Now it's a really easy place to live."

Over one summer, the couple worked like crazy. "It was an exciting time for us," Mia says. "We were moving in together, and we did everything ourselves. I learnt how to take out an oven and to paint." They also made some small alterations: taking out a door to increase the natural light, and puttying up dents in the walls. Steph's mum pitched in to paint the window frames, and a friend pulled out old carpet and replaced it with lino. In the kitchen they took out a gigantic, buzzing, grease-covered light fitting and removed some of the cabinets. "There was this one cupboard above the kitchen sink – a huge old-school fit-out that blocked a lot of light," Steph says. "When we talked about Mia moving in here, she was like, 'If I'm doing it, that cupboard has to go.' She just got up there on a ladder and I've never seen her with so much ferocity. She'd been waiting to rip it out for years."

As well as the renovations, Steph and Mia have brought together their furnishings to create a space that feels their own. "We both love hunting for things in op shops and junk stores," says Mia. Curtains in Steph's studio, for instance, are made of fabric she found in an op shop when the couple were visiting Mia's mum. "I was obsessed with it and wondered what I could do with it," Steph says. "Lo and behold, it's exactly the width of my window." The furniture in the living room is a combination of new purchases and touched-up hard rubbish, including the coffee table, which they stripped down and oiled up. "We've always had good-looking furniture," Mia says, "and usually it's just stuff we find. But recently we bought a proper, adult, comfy couch. It's our little secret, but we both really like watching TV, and now we stretch out in the evenings and relax on it. It's the best!"

Designwise, Mia and Steph have similar tastes, but they're divided on the question of whether less is more. "Mia grew up in a really cluttered environment – the type I love – and I grew up in a sparse type of house," Steph says. "Now I love clutter and Mia's much more of a minimalist." In their own house, they've managed to meet somewhere in the middle. In the living room, there are some sentimental pieces they've held onto for years, as well as friends' artworks they've acquired more recently. One of the older pieces, a small carousel, is especially meaningful to Mia. "My stepdad is a sculptor," she says, "and on the first day that we met, back when he was wooing my mum, he tried to win me over." He had made the 10-year-old horse fanatic a carousel with two horses that spin around the centre. "When he showed it to me, they were spinning so fast I couldn't see what they were, and he told me I had to guess before I could have it. That's a pretty special thing to me, and it's been in every house of mine ever since."

The baby's bedroom is still relatively spare, although that may change. "It's fun for us to have a whole new spectrum of things to hunt for," Mia says. "But it's funny when you're pregnant because there are these milestones that you have to hit, and it feels a bit tentative." Now they're on the home stretch, though, they're planning a working bee. "We have a huge cohort of people who'll be a big part of the baby's life," Steph says, "so they're going to come over and help to paint the room and decorate." They're excited to start their family in a home with so much history and love. "I've never gotten over how good this place is," Steph says. "But I think it's even better now that we've customised it. We love making stuff and turning things into our own, and I think if you have that attitude, you can live almost anywhere and still have fun." •

Above: Steph found the fabric for the curtains in her studio at an op shop.

Dawn & Andrew Lindsay

live in bayside Melbourne.
She is a burlesque artist; he is a
drummer & vintage car dealer.

WORDS KOREN HELBIG PHOTOGRAPHS OLGA BENNETT

From the street, Dawn and Andrew Lindsay's bayside Melbourne home doesn't look all that different from its neighbours: a brick and timber-clad affair with a modest front lawn sliced by a two-track concrete driveway. Certain things, though, do suggest something a bit special might be hiding within. The place is painted pastel yellow, for example, punctuated by a cherry red front door. An impressive cactus collection lines the side fence. And, should you roll up the garage door, you'll find a mint condition '69 Ford Ranch Wagon nestled beside the bones of an under-construction hot rod.

Turns out the Lindsays are obsessed with American mid-century modern style and, over the past two decades, have kitted out their 1948 three-bedroom home with treasures fossicked from that era. "We've both been heavily into the vintage aesthetic and rockin' scene for a long time," Dawn says. "I certainly wouldn't want to be a woman in the 1950s, but I'd love to step back in time and grab things from that era, particularly the music, movies, clubs and style."

The pair met through mutual friends, and cemented their own friendship after Andrew gatecrashed Dawn's 21st in the best possible way – with his band in tow, who promptly began playing for the crowd. (Andrew's still a professional drummer, playing internationally in rockabilly and rhythm and blues bands while dealing in vintage classic cars by day.) They got together in 1998 after Dawn moved from Sydney to Melbourne, where Andrew was already shacked up in the house they call home today.

The pair started renovating pretty much from day one, slowly amassing an enormous catalogue of vintage books and magazines for style tips. "We go through those and look at things that would suit our place," Dawn says. "My husband's attention to detail is fantastic and he's really good with colours."

That eye for colour was put to work indoors, with every room bar their master bedroom splashed with warm pastels. Dawn and Andrew mixed up the colours themselves,

referring to 1950s paint charts they rustled up at flea markets.

Decorating from such a colourful base might have made a more hesitant hand pause, but Dawn says their decision to focus mainly on 1950s furniture with a splash of 1940s Hawaiiana eased the way. "I know some people like to paint houses completely white, but we're not that kind of a couple."

Dawn dreams of getting her hands on more pieces by Heywood-Wakefield, the American furniture maker whose mid-century modern pieces are now highly sought-after collectibles, but says precious few make it over to Australia from the US. Dawn has only ever scored one 1950s chest of drawers imported by a Collingwood antique dealer, which now has pride of place in the master bedroom. "I just happened to walk in and purchased it on the spot," she recalls. "I've got all my lovely vintage sweaters, jewellery and make-up in there."

The Lindsays' fascination with vintage spills over into their clothing choices; their joint collection is now so large their western-themed guest bedroom has morphed into a giant wardrobe cum dressing room. That was partly necessitated by Dawn's decision, four years ago, to quit nursing and turn her part-time burlesque gig into a full-time affair. She now runs the Australian Burlesque Festival while also teaching and performing under the stage name Dolores Daiquiri – and has a multitude of elaborate stage costumes to show for it. Dawn often repairs them herself in the little office next door that doubles as her sewing room and Andrew's music room.

Sharing's not a problem, Dawn says, but sometimes she wishes they had extra room to house their growing vintage collection. "Unless it's a killer piece, we tend to hold off because we don't have the space. Generally, it will be me that finds a piece and Andrew will say, 'Sounds great but where will we put it?' He's pretty practical and I'm the shopper," she says. "When you find pieces, you get very excited. The chase is probably just as good as wearing or using the items."

Left page, below right:
The western-themed
guest bedroom also
doubles as a wardrobe
and dressing room.

→   121

←

That said, they haven't completely eschewed modern comforts. Their 1950s fridge has recently been relegated to the shed and many of their vintage appliances have been swapped for newer replicas. "In the early days I had an old toaster and an old kettle, but after a while you get sick of always burning the toast or the water boiling over," Dawn says.

They don't, however, plan on swapping to a more modern home any time soon, even though living in something built more than half a century ago has its downsides. The place needs loads of upkeep, and the Lindsays feel like they're constantly renovating and living in a work-in-progress. So far, they're most proud of their efforts in the kitchen, ditching the 1980s remodelling that most definitely did not fit their mid-century vibe. "We totally gutted it and designed a 1950s-style kitchen," says Dawn. "We just love it."

Outdoors, in a nod to California's Palm Springs, where mid-century modern arguably originated, Dawn has amassed a collection of about 60 cacti and succulents. "I just love that desert look, it sits well with our house," Dawn says. "Though I was out in the garden yesterday and I have a few war wounds, some scratches on my arms." Battle scars aside, Dawn loves the fact that cacti are mostly

Left page: One room doubles as Dawn's sewing room, where she repairs her costumes, and Andrew's music room.

self-caring, requiring only the odd spot of weeding and a dash of water here and there.

Elsewhere, the Lindsays have grand plans for more renos. Their crappy bathroom is first on the list – it's Dawn's pet hate – and the laundry, too. The rest, she says, is purely aesthetics. "We'll probably do a '50s-style carport and then the driveway and porch. We'd love a patio out the back of the house. So that's our plan for the next couple of years and then we can relax a bit more."

The hold-up is partly lack of time – Dawn travels a lot for her performances, while Andrew often hits the road with his band. And it takes time to fossick up the pieces they love so much. "We have a 1950s door that has a porthole with a swan in it, which took ages to find," Dawn says. "It's sitting in our garage for now and will go in our kitchen; we've just got to get around to resizing and fitting it."

Nonetheless, their mid-century obsession is a labour of love they can't imagine giving up. "We're both creative people, and I think our home is pretty much an extension of being artists," Dawn says. "A lot of our friends are into the same thing – the music, the cars, the clothes, the furniture. It's the whole lifestyle for us. To Andrew and I, this is normal." •

Previous page: Flooring at Alex Bennett and Tina Helm's house (photo by Olga Bennett).
Left: Fabric at Dawn and Andrew Lindsay's house (photo by Olga Bennett).
Above: Nataly Lee and Euan Gray's place (photo by Nataly Lee).
Next page: Sparkles in Rachel Burke's studio (photo by Natalie McComas).

Left: Abbey Rich's textile design hung over her sofa (photo by Olga Bennett).
Above: Abbey Rich's palette (photo by Olga Bennett).
Next page: Bathroom floor at Geordie Malone and Eartha Smith's house (photo by Saskia Wilson).

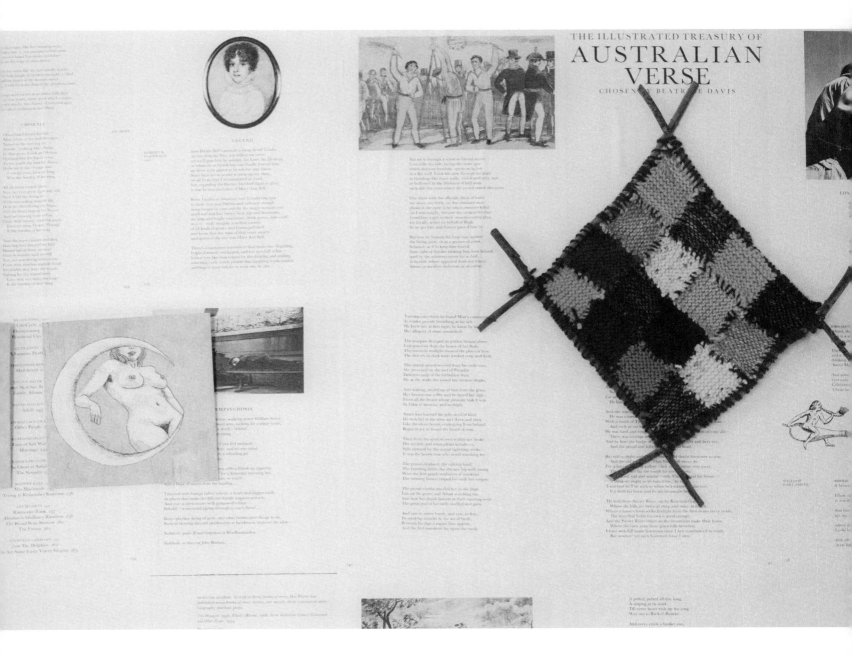

Left: Fabric in Ly Yeow's room (photo by Elvina Farkas).
Above: Detail of a wall in Hayley and Chadd Kessner's house (photo by Rachel Woods).
Next page: Flooring at Alex Bennett and Tina Helm's house (photo by Olga Bennett).

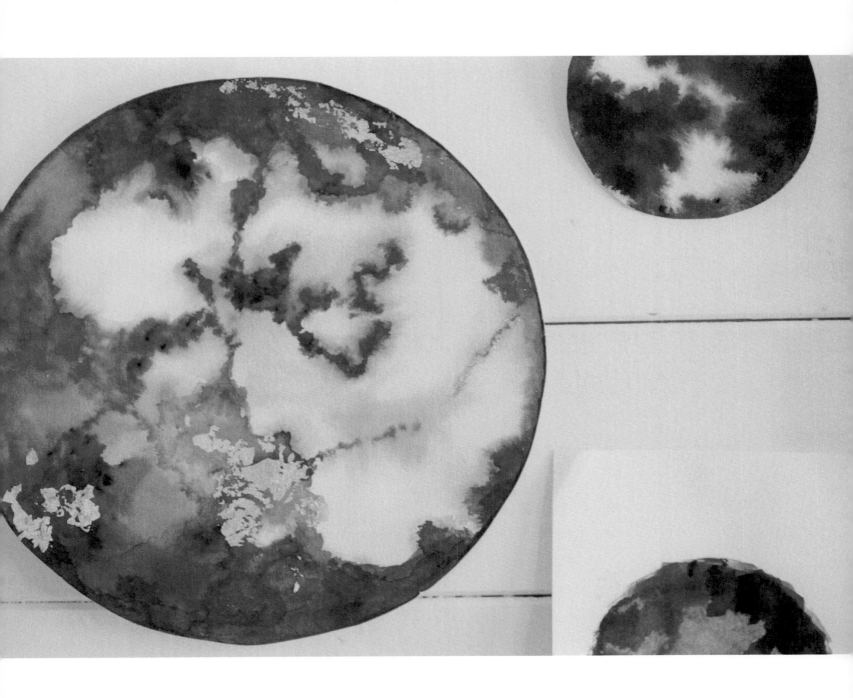

Left: Space mural on a ceiling at Alex Bennett and Tina Helm's house (photo by Olga Bennett).
Above: Detail of a wall in Hayley and Chadd Kessner's house (photo by Rachel Woods).
Next page: Chair at Laurie Melia and Rod Flynn's place (photo by Rachel Woods).

MABEL & IVY WINDRED-WORNES

LIVE WITH THEIR PARENTS &
LITTLE BROTHER IN NORTHCOTE,
MELBOURNE. THEY PLAY IN A FOLK
BAND, CHARM OF FINCHES.

INTERVIEWS MIA TIMPANO **PHOTOGRAPHS** HILARY WALKER

There's precious little space at the Windred-Wornes residence. Mabel, 17, has a room crammed with mum Jo's craft supplies; Ivy, 14, shares a space with little brother Percy. Meanwhile, Jo's desk is in the hallway, and the lounge room floor doubles as the kids' study area. But it's home. It's also where Mabel and Ivy pen their award-winning music.

The teenagers recall the O Brother, Where Art Thou? soundtrack playing in the background of their childhood "forever", their introduction to three-part harmonies and Americana folk. As Charm of Finches, they make the kind of tunes that wrap you in a blanket of stars. Highly respected in the independent music community, they've gigged with Clare Bowditch and toured Australia. They've lived in the Northcote family home all their lives.

MABEL // BIG SISTER

What makes your room uniquely yours? It's my space. I used to be in a room with my sister. Then I kicked Mum and Dad out of the study and made it into my room. I have all my books and instruments in here. It's nice when the sun comes in during the afternoon. I've got these crystal things hanging on the window, so little rainbows shine on the wall.

You've got a lot of cool stuff. What are you proudest of? Probably my paintings and drawings. I'm quite into art. I've also got a big mock cheque from when we won the Darebin songwriting competition.

How did you decide who got to keep the cheque? Well, strictly speaking, I won the competition, because it was my song, so I got to keep the cheque – but I don't think Ivy minds too much.

Do you spend much time in each other's rooms? Yeah. I think Ivy comes into my room more than I go into hers, because she's a bit like, "Get off my bed. Can you get out now?" She's quite protective of her space, I think more than me. We often practise in here, and do home recordings.

What are the acoustics like? It's pretty dead, so the acoustics aren't great, but that's where you just put a bit of reverb in and you're fine.

How did your band, Charm of Finches, come into existence? Well, we're sisters, so we've been playing music together forever. In grade six, I wrote a song about druids because I'd read a book about Celtic druids. Then I just kept writing songs and we started playing gigs around Australia. We do lots of folk festivals. Recently, we got a whole heap of songs together and made an album. That's where we are now.

IVY // LITTLE SISTER

You and Mabel used to share a room... It was really hard, because we had different tastes in music. We'd also argue sometimes, but that's the way it is with all siblings. Now I can spread out a bit more, but I still have to share my room with my brother, Percy. He doesn't sleep in my room, but all his stuff is in there. It's a little annoying, because he pulls it out and leaves it there. He's got toys, books, games and blankets for cubbies.

Does he like Charm of Finches' music? I think when we started he did, but now I think he's a little bit sick of us, because he's heard us a lot.

What's your songwriting process? Usually Mabel writes a song and then brings it to me; I add the harmonies. But sometimes I come into her room and we sit down on her bed, write a song and record it on the iPhone.

Is there anything in your room that makes you especially happy? Probably my furry blanket. When I come home from school, I lie on it, on my bed. It looks like a tiger. It was my dad's and I stole it from him because I liked it so much. He didn't care. I think I like it more than he does.

JO // MUM

How do the girls go at keeping their rooms clean? Much better than I do. If it comes down to doing something creative for fun or doing boring cleaning, I'll always pick the fun thing. This shoot's been good, because we've been like, "We better clean the windows, they'll need light in here!" Percy and I were out there this afternoon, giving the windows a bit of a scrub. Not part of the regular regime, but for art, we'll do it. •

Josh Barnes &
Emma Schuberg Barnes

live in Katoomba in the NSW
Blue Mountains. Josh is a community
entrepreneur; Emma is a visual art
teacher & installation artist.

WORDS LETA KEENS PHOTOGRAPHS SASKIA WILSON

Chance plays a part in everyone's lives, including Josh Barnes'. He'd headed up to the Blue Mountains from Sydney a few years ago, and bumped into a friend who asked if he could look after his house for a while. It sounded like a good idea, especially as his love life in the city was a disaster at the time.

While Josh was house-sitting, he wandered past a real estate agency and noticed an ad, low down in the window. 'Studio in Nature', it read. He'd been trying to set up a co-op outside the city with a few people, but the idea hadn't taken off; the studio, which he could buy on his own, seemed a better option. It was, for a number of reasons, not least of which was the turnaround in his love life. He probably wouldn't have met his wife, Emma, without it. "Her aunt has a property next door, and Emma used to come up and stay sometimes."

When Josh, who was brought up in North Queensland, first got hold of The Hut, it wasn't much more than a shed. "Other people would have knocked it down," he says. "I wanted a project, a place I could play with and make mistakes with." A caravan he put on site was the only solid thing about the property; water ran through the shack, and most of it was eaten out by white ants. There was no running water or electricity in what was once a shed for livestock.

But the setting was a winner – on a steep site in the middle of a gum forest, with a creek at the bottom of the land. "It's like looking out on a Frederick McCubbin painting," says Emma. "And being able to hear the creek and the frogs and the birds is outstanding." An American must have surveyed the region – the creek they hear is called Coyote Creek; the whole area is known as Yosemite Valley.

Josh's first go at renovating was to make a retreat for himself – somewhere he could spend time in, but not necessarily a permanent home. When he and Emma first got together, they weren't there all the time, either – they moved between each other's places, and also worked up in Darwin for a while. When they weren't in their mountain retreat, they rented it out on Airbnb, and part

of the business Josh has built up in the Blue Mountains is to advise others on how to set up their houses for short-term rentals.

Originally, he created one large open space: bedroom, living room and kitchen together, with an outdoor shower. Since he and Emma set up house more permanently, he has completely reworked the place. "I loved it the way it was, and felt sick about changing it," he says, "but it didn't work to live in." Adds Emma: "It was a lovely retro bush experience, but it's much more functional now." With its insulation and woodburning stove, The Hut is also, she says, "honestly the warmest place I've ever lived – Josh doesn't like being cold."

In its new configuration, the bedroom is now separate from the living room, and the shower is indoors – in an odd but clever location. It's in a corridor-like arrangement just inside the front door – shower at one end, washbasin at the other, with one wall a clear screen and huge window, with pot plants, facing onto the driveway. Given that one of the things Josh loves about the mountains is the habit friends have of dropping in on each other, "that's a bit of a problem!" Not that it bothers Emma. "The bathroom is my favourite moment of this version of the house. I like the idea of a bathhouse among lots of greenery and ferns, and the idea of recycling water for that use."

Over the years Josh has spent fixing The Hut, he's learnt he's a "pretty average carpenter", but has occasionally called for help along the way. "I'm a gardener and have always used my hands – my grandfather was very handy, my father not at all, so I used to do the things Dad wouldn't do." An Irish backpacker with some carpentry training helped with basic building work, using mainly recycled materials. At first, Josh picked up anything that came his way but, without a plan, discovered he was "constantly moving shit around". Sometimes that worked. Windows, which originally would have hung vertically, have been placed on their side high up on the back wall of the shack to provide a framed view up the hill. "I knew I wanted windows there, but would have spent ages angsting over their design – I got these and put them in, and they look just right."

The Hut has its own time. You experience what it's like to be not so plugged in all the time.

←

Over time, he became increasingly choosy and just picked up bits and pieces for various projects – the orange '60s doors from a university building that now, ingeniously, make up part of one wall of the shack; the rusty old tin that clads the wall dividing the kitchen from the bedroom. He loved the colour of the tin, but wasn't so keen on it being corrugated; he sorted that out one night in a local car park, first sweeping the bitumen to get rid of any rocks, then laying down the sheets and driving backwards and forwards over them in his four-wheel drive for an hour. "I tried it with the sheets on top of each other, and that didn't work," he says. "I had to do them all individually."

That wall contains one of Josh's favourite new additions – the tea tap. With the sink on the back wall, a few steps away from the main part of the kitchen, the tap means "you don't have to walk far to make a cup of tea – I'm very proud of it." He removed the cladding to install the tap, and never put it back. "It gives a bit of shelving and more space without it." Emma describes the evolution of The Hut as "a work of ongoing inspiration".

Another addition to the place, in the back corner, is a tiny dressing room for Emma, hidden behind a New Guinea wall hanging that was a gift from a friend whose stuff Josh has been looking after for years. "I love that he thought about that area for me," she says. There's also a walk-in pantry up that end of the house which, with its window facing onto the living area ("I ran out of floorboards so shoved it in"), looks more like a shed than anything else. Above that, there's a guest bedroom. "That works really well – it's so warm up there," says Josh.

The furniture is a mix of family heirlooms, things Josh has had for ages, various bits and pieces he's minding for friends, and others he's picked up along the way. The dining table, for instance, was an engagement present to

his great-grandparents in 1919; Josh bought the chest of drawers in the bedroom when he first left home; a trunk in the bedroom belonged to a friend's grandmother; and the kitchen workbench was inherited from a share house he used to live in. The food warmer, used for storage, doesn't work anymore, "but certain things grab me. Mrs Hunter in the film *The Eye of the Storm* has one."

While in many ways, the house has everything anyone would need, the fact that it's off-grid makes Josh and Emma live in a different way. "It has its own time," she says. "You experience what it's like to not be so plugged in all the time." As there's no mains electricity, lighting is never bright. "We tend to decharge in the evening and I think that's really healthy," says Josh. "And having an outside toilet means you're forced to go out into the elements – you come out of your warm comfortable space and notice what the weather's doing." As well, it's a house in which "we can hear every sound of each other, so you have to be really respectful. I have a very gentle and considerate wife, whereas I'm probably the loud one."

How long they will be there is anyone's guess – they have thoughts of spending time back up in the Northern Territory. "But even then, this will be our place," says Josh. "I met a lovely Kiwi man once who used the word *türangawaewae*, which is about custodianship and your place to come back to. This is it."

Postscript: A few days before we went to print, we had an email from Josh to tell us he and Emma had been forced to leave The Hut. The local council told them it didn't comply with building standards. Josh said, on one level, he understood, but was frustrated by "the narrow definitions of the ways that spaces are officially understood". We agree with him. The last line of his email read: "I hope that you will still run the story of The Hut." We didn't hesitate for a minute; we loved The Hut when we first saw it, and we love it even more now. •

*Left page, top right:
Part of one wall in The Hut
is made of '60s orange
doors, recycled from a
university building.*

Patrick Floyd Meade

lives in a house called the Sugar
Shack in Venus Bay, Victoria.
He is a designer & maker.

WORDS DANIEL EVANS PHOTOGRAPHS MARNIE HAWSON & BECKIE LITTLER

"When you think about it, we are fluid museums. We hold experiences and memories, and covet objects that remind us of who we are, or were, and what we admire," says Patrick Floyd Meade. "Not to get too hippy about it, but there is a vibe or energy around certain objects or pieces of furniture. It's nice to think about being a custodian of these things for a little while, not quite knowing where they've been, or maybe where they'll end up."

Paddy is a collector who loves the neglected, which is all part of his "nostalgic heart", he says. He lives in Melbourne during the week, but found a dilapidated two-storey house on Victoria's Gippsland coast to transform into a retreat studded with salvaged wares.

"It might look a little ramshackle but it's quite considered," Paddy says. "I'd collect materials during the week and bring them here on the weekend. I'd fix them up as I saw fit. Place them in that corner, or by that window. I love minimalism as well, but I pick up things a bit more than a minimalist ever would."

Paddy doesn't set out to look for things, he says. "This stuff just finds me. I'll walk down the street and go, 'Ow!' and I've hit my knee on a chair. And then some other piece will hit me in the back of the head. I get home, I shake myself off and find half a house of furniture."

The result is a patchwork of aesthetics that shift and bend between – and even within – rooms. The kitchen/living/dining area, for instance, mixes it up with a chandelier, chunky timber furniture and '50s kitchen cupboards. And on the ground floor is Paddy's studio space, fitted out with salvaged steel-framed windows. Alongside artworks by various friends, there's his 1946 Bondwood caravan, Lucky. He picked it up from a guy who had wanted to restore it but only got as far as taking off the outside skin. "He couldn't find the time to finish it and, thankfully, hadn't touched the inside," Paddy says. "I bought it to use as a bedroom in a warehouse I lived in at the time. Now it's on permanent vacation." To compensate for the lack of an outside skin, he wallpapered the exterior with Chinese paper.

It took two years' of working bees to renovate the house, which Paddy calls the Sugar Shack. "I've freelanced for a long time, so have a great network of mates who would come down and help me out. Some got paid. Some got beer. In the end, I let most of them stay for their own holidays." He doesn't charge anyone for going down there, and all his friends know where the keys are hidden.

"I wanted to create that feeling that you can walk straight in, drop your stuff and do whatever you want," says Paddy. "In our chaotic world, we need that space to let what we do, day in, day out, go for a few days."

Around three hours from Melbourne, the only thing missing from the Sugar Shack is "some sort of teleportation device to cut down the travel time", but Paddy says the trip is definitely worthwhile. "In a world of billions of people, you often find you have the whole beach to yourself. I have swum with seals, and it's also home to migratory birds nesting in the dunes from as far away as Siberia. There are even claims of Tasmanian tiger sightings."

The appreciation for the place extends beyond his circle of friends. "One weekend I opened the door and found a note from the daughter of the guy who built it," Paddy says. "It said she was so fearful of coming around the corner and seeing it destroyed or abandoned. But there it was, as she remembered, with a few improvements, even!"

Now that the Sugar Shack is complete, Paddy is turning his attention to an old church on the outskirts of Bangalow in northern New South Wales. From here he'll run his bespoke furniture business, where he's just finished redesigning and building studio easels for the Victorian College of the Arts. There's talk of vintage-inspired colouring books for adults and some wooden puzzle games.

"Let's embrace the future in a way that celebrates quality and encourages longevity. I think if you can appreciate the craft of an object, its history, we might take more care with it; and more care, for any one thing – big or small – is never bad." •

Sam James, Emma Finneran
& Matt Bromhead
live above a Greek Orthodox
church in Surry Hills, Sydney.
They are all artists.

WORDS LETA KEENS PHOTOGRAPHS SASKIA WILSON

There's a certain rhythm to life when you live above a church. While the rest of the world manages a lie-in on a Sunday morning, it's an early start at Sam James, Emma Finneran and Matt Bromhead's place. First, there are the bells. "I've never been able to work out whether they're to say the service is starting or it's over, even after all this time," says Sam, who's been living there for four years, and whose bedroom was padded when he moved in. "That must have been the previous tenant's attempt at soundproofing, but I don't see how it could have worked. It looked quite eerie." Then there's the chanting. "No hymn singing from the congregation," he says. "It's just one or two men chanting, that's it."

After that, the smells start wafting up from the kitchen. You'd expect moussaka or maybe some lamb, but the overwhelming smell is always of fish fingers. "The frankincense makes up for it," says Sam. "That lasts all through Sunday, Monday and Tuesday." When the congregation is in a particularly festive mood, they'll set up a PA system and, says Matt, "play Zorba, and they'll be stomping". Occasionally, there will be "little market stalls with pickles and jams out the front of the church", says Emma.

The apartment is essentially one long room with a bedroom at either end, behind low-ish partition walls, and a kitchen off to the side. With an alleyway running behind it, Saturday nights close to Taylor Square and Oxford Street, in Sydney's Surry Hills, can be rowdy. Then, occasionally, comes the sound, "chooka chooka ssshhhh – someone graffitiing in the alley", says Emma.

However, in daylight hours, during the week, the only thing you can hear is the benign sound of kids at play in the local primary school. "And there's so much light and air that it feels as if you're half outside – you can stay here all day and not get cabin fever," says Matt.

The wide-open views from the living area windows are pretty unexpected in the middle of the city. "We used to live in a top floor flat near the beach in Bronte and didn't see as much sky," says Emma. "We're only up one

flight of stairs, but see people's rooftops, which is nice. It's the perfect spot really."

It may only be one flight of stairs, but they're possibly the steepest steps in Sydney, and just right for a church – they're like ones that go up to a bell tower rather than a two-bedroom flat, with the biggest living space around. "We had Emma's sister's 30th birthday here," says Matt. "It was so beautiful – we gutted the entire place and filled it with tables. We've had some pretty memorable parties here, but nowhere near as often as we should – we should be having them all the time."

When Sam moved in four years ago after two of his friends saw a "straightforward real estate ad" for 'a unique space', there was a bit of work to be done to liven the place up. "It was a yukky yellowy colour, so we painted the whole thing," he says. "The oven and sink were already there in the kitchen, but my old housemates also put benches and shelves in there – they were much handier than me."

While it may well have been an apartment for some time, how it was originally used is a bit of a mystery. One of Sam's bedroom doors, opening onto the back stairway down to the parish kitchen, is split in two across the middle like a stable door. It's anyone's guess as to what that was for.

When Sam's original flatmates were moving out, he texted a few people he knew to try to find new housemates. One was Emma, who had worked with Sam at a café, and had been to the flat before. "I had to coax Matt to come and look at it," she says. "We had been living at the beach and he thought Taylor Square was too noisy. But once he saw it, we did everything in our powers to convince Sam that we should move in."

Taylor Square may still not be Matt's favourite place on the planet, but the apartment itself and its sense of isolation won him over. "It's so peaceful here that walking out at certain times of day, right into the middle of Taylor Square, can be quite a jolt," he says. The space itself, says Emma, feels neutral: "If it felt eerie or churchy, I wouldn't be able to live here."

*All the furniture's a bit
junky, which we like.
We have about five
lounges, which is a bit
of an issue when there
are only three of us.*

The furniture in the flat is a mix of stuff all three of them have picked up along the way, along with a few bits and pieces left by the church, including an enormous dining table and some pews. The other dining chairs are ones that Matt snared after an auction sale at a country property.

"All the furniture's a bit junky, which we like," says Emma, who also moves things around pretty regularly. "We have about five lounges, which is a bit of an issue when there are only three of us. I worked out once there are about 40 spots to sit. My mum timed me when I moved in to see how long it would take me to sit in every seat in the place, and it took about a minute."

Despite having a huge dining table, they rarely eat together. "I always have these beautiful plans of saying we should have a Sunday roast, and get all inspired, but never do anything about it," says Emma. "We've got pissed a few times when we've ended up back here after being in different spots."

Artwork is their own, or swaps they have done with friends. "Matt's and my works are big, and we've never had a chance to live with them before. In any other circumstances, they'd all be stacked up, but because we have the wall space here, we can hang them."

She and Sam both use the flat to work in; Matt has his studio in Alexandria. "I like it when Emma's playing music," says Sam. "If I don't like the music, I just put headphones on. Plus, I really like having people around when I'm working." And, "I'm the same," says Emma.

Cleaning and household chores are not equally shared among the housemates. Sam describes himself as being "pretty pathetic" at such things. "I'm like a live-in house fairy," says Emma. "Some people are like, 'You should tell Matt to clean up after himself more.' For some reason it doesn't bother me. I'm the one who moves shit around, I'm the one who likes things to look good. I've always been like that – my mother is one of the untidiest people I know, and so is my sister, and growing up with them, my room was always perfect. If I'm painting, I'll say I'm going to stop and sweep now."

Living above the church isn't without its challenges. There's the "funky" shower room downstairs. "It's fine if you're used to it, but when it gets feral, you have to clean it with a broom," says Emma. "I put on a hazmat one day." And then, annoyingly, the council doesn't allocate the apartment any garbage bins, says Sam. "Even though this place is perfectly legal, they can't get it together." So it's a case of "borrowing" other people's bins or "nicking them in the dead of night". And putting them out is no fun either. "On a Sunday night, it's the last thing you want to do, drag them right around the block," says Emma. "That's the only thing that sucks about cleaning here."

It's not great, either, that the place has no insulation, says Emma, "so you look as if you're in Jindabyne in winter and on an island beach in summer, but you get used to it." But it's always cool in the alleyway between the front gate and the front door, "and that's a really nice place to have a barbecue and hang out". The bathroom being downstairs is a real downer in winter. "I really wanted to get a bedpan," says Emma.

But it's hard to care about such things when you're living in one of the most unexpected places in Sydney. Probably the worst thing about it for Matt is that he and Emma like to move around a bit, "but this is just too good to give up. It's one of those places, that whatever happens, we'll end up thinking back to it, and how rare it is, and how unusual it was to live here." •

*Left, below right:
Paintings by Matt lean
on the bedroom wall.
Following page, above:
Works by Keith Haring
and Sam James hang in
Sam's bedroom. Below:
Sam's photos outside
his bedroom door.*

Katia Carletti & Rohan Fraser
live with their rabbit, Tilvie,
in Nailsworth, Adelaide. Katia is
a ceramicist; Rohan is an artist.

WORDS KOREN HELBIG **PHOTOGRAPHS** BRI HAMMOND

Katia Carletti and Rohan Fraser describe their suburban Adelaide rental as a "rambling mess". They can't shut their side gate because the cedar tree's grown wild under the house, skewing the pavers. And their bath is a no-go zone – Rohan used it just once and flooded the dining room. "That's because the fig tree is clogging the pipes," Katia says. Still, over the past four years, the couple has managed to spend almost nothing on a series of small changes that have transformed the place into a comfortable home and shared art studio, packed with Rohan's paintings, Katia's handmade pottery and a mix of thrifted and found furniture.

Katia and Rohan met in 2009 at Adelaide Central School of Art and later lived together for a year in a share house before Katia headed over to Iceland for an artist residency. When she got back in 2012, the couple decided to get their own place. It was actually the same runaway garden that gives the house so much structural grief that sealed the deal. "It was November and the lemon tree was going crazy with so many lemons," Katia says. "We didn't really think we could afford it because we're poor artists, but we just knew we had to get it. We got lucky."

The 100-year-old house was pretty shabby when they moved in, but they could see it had potential and enough space to double as a home studio. They imagined commandeering the front two bedrooms as their studios, with Rohan painting from one and Katia making pottery from the other. After a big clean-up, they gave the rattiest rooms a lick of paint, painting over the ugly brown kitchen cabinets and swapping the depressing deep green walls in Katia's studio for white. They also pulled down and replaced the crappy lace curtains adorning every window. "When it gets really hot I use them to drape over my tomato plants, so they're still getting used," Katia says. "They kind of look like ghosts, especially at night-time."

That's as far as they went with changes, because it didn't seem worth dropping any more cash on renos for a rental. Making the place feel like home then came down to well

Left page: An Ikea cabinet was repurposed to make a three-storey hutch for Tilvie the rabbit.

chosen furniture and splashes of art. The only problem was, they had no money and hardly any possessions, which meant styling the place was an evolving process. "Everything was either given to us or found on the side of the road or in op shops," Katia says of how their home came together. Her favourite find is a hand-carved wooden cabinet she stumbled on one morning while walking to her parents' house. "I sat by the side of the road and called my brother to come and get it with his station wagon, and was shooing people away because everyone wanted it!" she says. The wooden trunk in their living room was a hard rubbish score, too. "It was painted dark green and Rohan hated it because it's really heavy, but my dad restored it for us and it's so beautiful now," Katia says.

While op shop finds mostly filled their kitchen cupboards at first, Katia's gradually replaced the crockery with an ever-revolving collection of her own pottery pieces. "Most of it is just seconds that I can't really sell. There are a few pieces that I really like, but most of them have a chip or crack or something and I do eventually get rid of them as new, nicer cracked bits come in," she says. Likewise, Rohan's work is scattered throughout the house, and they've managed to get their hands on more art via swaps with friends or other artists. "Artist swaps are a good way of having nice things, especially when you probably couldn't afford them yourself. It's like an alternative currency," Katia says.

Last year, though, Katia and Rohan decided to splash out on the most expensive thing they'd ever bought for their home: a kiln in the back shed. It was a huge decision, and installation set them back a couple of thousand dollars, but it's made Katia's life a whole lot easier. Before, she'd deliberately enrolled in the same glaze and kiln subject at TAFE each semester just to have access to the school's kiln. "I would take my pots and fire them and just do my own thing," she says. "Both my parents are art teachers so I was using the kiln at my mum's school as well. I was driving pots all over town, these fragile, unfired things, and it was a bit of a nightmare. It's great to have it all at one place now."

←

*Above, right: Behind
Katia is the hand-carved
wooden cabinet she
stumbled on when she
was going to her parents'
house one morning.*

Katia says she loves working from home, especially now that her day is organised around the slow processes of clay drying and kiln firing. It forces her to take regular breaks, which she puts to good use by pottering around the garden or making bread.

Every now and then it can get just a little bit lonely, though, especially when Rohan's at work – he lectures on art part-time at TAFE – but that's where their little rabbit Tilvie comes in. "It's just nice to have a little creature to say hi to here and there," Katia says. Tilvie has free range of the house and garden by day and sleeps in an Ikea cabinet repurposed into a three-storey hutch at night. She's only banned from the bedroom, both to prevent her revenge-peeing on Rohan's pillow and keep her from chewing expensive MacBook chargers. "That's her one vice," Katia says. "She really is very sweet. She just follows you around and gives you constant licks, and loves to snuggle for many hours. It's the main perk of working from home."

Katia says their neighbourhood, Nailsworth, about four kilometres north of Adelaide's CBD, isn't much to rave about – a quiet and relatively cheap area that's mainly home to families and retirees. "On the opposite side of the main road, the houses are a bit bigger, the streets a bit wider, the trees a bit bigger and it's really gorgeous and expensive. Our side is the slightly smaller, shabbier side," she says. But Rohan's work is close by and Katia's parents live just three streets away, which has its perks. "Usually I can pop round there on the weekend or my sister rides her bike over to help me do pots," she says. "Mum left some eggs on the front doorstep last week from a friend at work, so that was nice. We're not super attached to this area but I have lived here pretty much my whole life so I guess it's just homely and feels familiar."

But their time in Nailsworth, or this rental house at least, could soon come to an end. Rohan and Katia have been slowly saving to buy their own place, and hope to make the move sometime after getting married in April this year. For his part, Rohan says he'll be happy to give Katia free rein to decorate again in the future. "I'm definitely thankful Katia took the initiative, because I'm inspired by the space," Rohan says. "I've got paintings that I've done as a response to this space. The light is really good, so it's good to set up arrangements, which usually have some of Katia's work in them or her plants, or maybe little food scenes. I respond to this space more than I add to it. It's nice to feel inspired without even having to leave your own home." •

A BUNCH OF PEOPLE WORK TOGETHER AT NICHOLSON STREET STUDIOS IN BRUNSWICK EAST, MELBOURNE.

INTERVIEWS CHRIS HARRIGAN **PHOTOGRAPHS** HILARY WALKER

Wedding Albums
Passports
Commercial
Colour

Usually, when a couple starts thinking about going into business together, they're given a piece of unsolicited advice: don't. But for the four romantic and professional duos in Melbourne's Nicholson Street Studios – who make up eight of the 10 occupants – things just seem to work. Perhaps it has something to do with the space. Set up by Hilary Walker and her husband Benjamin Baldwin, the large, open-plan office somehow channels the right mix of calm and creativity. The best evidence that it all works? The single tenants don't even seem to mind being outnumbered.

HILARY WALKER //
PHOTOGRAPHER & STUDIO OWNER

Ben and I were looking for a space we could live in, where he could also set up a workshop for his woodwork. I had to be talked into it, but when I saw how awesome this place would be for my photography work, it made sense to do it.

I kind of freaked out when we moved in. The place was just a big brick shell with a pitched roof; a real warehouse, very bare bones. But it's a playful space, too. I used to ride my bike inside, and we had our wedding reception here, with a big party in the open space. When we had our baby, we decided to move into a normal house. We always had ideas about turning this place into a shared workspace, so we bit the bullet and spent about six months renovating. Ben's a perfectionist and wanted to do it himself, so he'd do it in the evenings after work.

We've kept the decor quite minimal. We wanted it to feel like a blank slate for people to move into. The first time we gave anyone the keys it felt a bit funny. I thought, "Oh, it's not our house anymore." But now we want people to like it so much they don't want to leave.

BENJAMIN BALDWIN //
FURNITURE MAKER &
STUDIO OWNER

It was pretty rough when we moved in; no insulation, no cooling. But it had beautiful natural light, so we put a lot of energy into making it comfortable. I work for Sea Shepherd by day, fixing their vessels and assisting with operations around Australia, so I spent my afternoons and evenings either setting up the place, or in my workshop, making recycled furniture.

Eventually, we started looking at other ways to use the space. We knew other people were looking for places like this to work in, so it just made sense. Hilary had a lot to say about how the studio would look, and I did more of the hands-on stuff. We installed a claw foot bath in the middle of the room, which was our shower. It's still there, but now it's full of plants, and doubles as a cooler if we're having parties.

It was a little odd, no longer having full ownership of the warehouse, but I prefer it now. It really feels like a collaborative space. We don't feel like landlords. We feel more like family.

ERIN KING //
SENIOR PRODUCER,
99 PRODUCTIONS

My husband, Andrew, and I produce advertising campaigns. We do a lot of casting for models, and use the studio at the back to take photos. Some are high-end international models, at other times we need "real" people. If I'm at a shopping centre or a sports event and see somebody really unique, I give them my card.

We love working here. It's the little things: the floors, the tiles, the furniture. I don't know where Hilary finds it all. We're in the two little offices at the front, just a stone's throw from everyone in the main space. We wanted to join a space where there were other creative people, but which would still give us a bit of privacy so we don't distract them. It's the perfect balance.

We work in a demanding and fast-paced industry. But when we walk into Hilary and Ben's studio, we instantly feel calm. It's not just because it's huge and bright. It's the people. They're so kind and smart, and they make us relax. Andrew and I really need that sometimes.

**ANDREW ZAPPIA //
SENIOR PRODUCER,
99 PRODUCTIONS**

Erin and I love working together.
I can understand how some couples
would struggle with it, but we get
along really well. We challenge
and push and really complement
each other.

Before this, we were working at
an office in Fitzroy, but decided
we wanted a fresh start. Basically,
we wanted to work with more
creative people. The mix here is
just right. Everyone is a bit more
established, both professionally and
at home, than the people at a lot of
other shared studios. It has a really
nice, relaxed vibe, and it's neat that
we can bring in our kids from time
to time, just to hang out for a bit.

We've got the best of both worlds
with our workspace, as well. The high
ceilings, the greenery, the natural
light; it just doesn't feel like you're
stuck in an office. Most importantly,
we were able to find a place where we
can close ourselves off when we're
making lots of loud phone calls, and
then we can integrate with everyone
in the shared space as well, have a
chat or an after-work drink. It's
everything we wanted.

**LILLI WATERS //
PHOTOGRAPHER**

It's nicer than any studio I've
ever worked in. Ben and Hilary
have managed to make it more like
a house. You come up two sets of
brick stairs and it's all white walls,
a couch, some chairs and plants,
and a cute little kitchen and dining
table. And it's all one big open plan,
so everyone can see each other, which
is nice. I have a studio at home, but I
don't work there very often because
I go a bit mad when I'm on my own all
day long. My husband gets home and
I'm hyperactive, because I haven't
spoken to anyone all day.

It's slowly filling up with more
people, which hopefully means more
movie nights or Friday night beers.
When I moved in, we had a party to
get to know each other. The people
with babies all went home early,
but the rest of us drank way too much
gin and ended up doing cartwheels
on the floor. We don't party too much,
though. Sometimes Ben will sit down
at the piano in the main room. When
I'm working late, I'll just sit there
and listen to him play.

**STEPHANIE PAJIC //
CO-FOUNDER, HOMECAMP
& UNDER SKY**

Doron and I run two businesses:
one is Homecamp, an online store.
The other is Under Sky, where we set
up glamping-style accommodation
for weddings and festivals. We were
engaged when we started Homecamp.
Now we're married and have a kid.
It's been a big couple of years.

We met Hilary at a party in the
country where we were setting up
tents, and forged a friendship. Back
then we were working from home,
but I'm more productive when I'm
around other people, so we jumped
at the chance to move in.

There are a few photographers
here, which makes sense: there's
a little photo studio out the back,
which is handy for us, as we're
constantly taking photos of products
for the website. We're all quite like-
minded people. I can see us all being
friends in the future. We're all on a
similar page, which is a testament
to Hilary attracting the right people
into the space.

It's a pleasure to walk in the door
every day. There's just an energy
you can't get when you're working
by yourself. Also, because Doron and
I alternate our days in the studio,
we get some breathing space from
each other. That can be nice.

DORON FRANCIS //
CO-FOUNDER, HOMECAMP
& UNDER SKY

Ben's done such an amazing job converting this place. It was just a big old empty Victorian-era building when they got here. And Hilary's done a really good job with the styling, too. It's got north-facing windows, so we get light that comes streaming through pretty much all day. It's pretty eclectic in terms of the furniture: there's a piano next to my desk. After a few beers, inevitably someone will give it a go.

The main thing for me is being around people who are busy and inspiring, and everyone here is really great and creative, with similar temperaments. I think a lot of that's due to Hilary: she's very thoughtful, and thinks a lot about who's coming in to stay. Not in a snobbish way; it's just all about people gelling together, isn't it?

Nearly everyone, like us, has kids. That really helps, because you're all on the same page. There was even a suggestion that we start our own crèche, where we all take turns looking after the kids. I like that.

TIM WATTERS //
CO-FOUNDER, FAIR PROJECTS

I run Fair Projects with my partner, Eliza Muirhead. It provides NGOs with professional-quality film, photography and graphic design. We figured if big companies can afford to get good media, the groups that are trying to save the climate or help those in need should have the option as well.

We did a lot of work for Sea Shepherd years ago, which is where I met Ben. We used to come round and hang out at his place, and we just loved the space. The way they laid it out was straight from my interior design dreams, so, of course, we were the first people to sign up when they turned it into a studio.

We don't have a baby, but we do have a rescue dog named Anoushka who comes for half the day. She's always walking around, having a peep at everything. The energy here is just fantastic. Ben and Hilary have such a good eye for design. It's spacious and calm, and the natural light is just famous. Often open-plan offices can be pretty chaotic and crammed, but there's so much space here. We haven't even explored it all yet.

CHARLIE KINROSS //
PHOTOGRAPHER

Years ago, I was working as a graphic designer when my cousin won a camera. He didn't want it, so I bought it off him and started taking pictures. I quickly discovered how much I loved it. I was good friends with Hilary, who's an exceptional photographer, and got her to mentor me. Eventually, I decided to start doing it professionally.

I knew the space from when Hilary lived here, so I understood how good it was for doing photography. The lunch table is my favourite spot; it's so large and rustic, and I've ended up doing a few portraits there. I like to have a nice outlook where I work, so I chose my spot in the main space carefully. I sit in the corner, facing the whole room, and I've got a nice bookshelf behind me, for inspiration.

As for Brunswick East, the area took a bit of getting used to. There are so many good cafés and shops around, but the aesthetic is a bit rough. You've just got to look a bit harder to find the beauty in it. I guess that just makes the studio all the more important. It feels like an oasis. •

Ophelia Mikkelson & Ryder Jones
live, create and play in Tairua,
New Zealand. They are artists.

WORDS LUCY CORRY PHOTOGRAPHS BENJAMIN & ELISE

Ophelia Mikkelson and Ryder Jones tell each other that one day they will live in a house with a view of the sea where they can watch the sun turn the water to liquid gold. For now, though, they realise they're onto a good thing. "We can't see the sea from our house, though we can hear it," Ophelia says. "Actually, we're doing pretty well. We will be lying in bed and Ryder will say, 'The waves sound like they might be big, I better go and have a look.'"

The couple – he's a sculptor and designer, she's a sock maker, spatial designer and photographer – live in a '70s surfie beach shack in the small coastal settlement of Tairua on New Zealand's Coromandel Peninsula. "The proximity to the ocean and being submerged in nature is our favourite thing about living here," Ophelia says. "Ryder surfs a lot and we try to swim all year round. We feel really, really lucky to be able to walk through our front yard and be on the beach." Adds Ryder: "I love to wake up early and go down to the dunes to watch the sun rise. That's probably my favourite thing about living here."

"We are super-fortunate to live here," Ophelia says. "For about two weeks of the year it's really busy, but most of the time we can walk down the beach and not see anyone. It's quite dreamlike." Every time Ryder goes to the beach, she says, "He makes me a necklace from things he finds. Sometimes I can wear them, sometimes they're so fragile that I pin them to the wall. They are all really beautiful, I treasure them."

They've lived in this spot for just over a year, long enough to see last year's plants regenerate in their well-tended vegetable plot and to put down their own roots in the little community. The move to Tairua was something of a homecoming for Ryder, who moved there with his family from Hawaii when he was in his early teens. Ophelia, who grew up in Auckland, used to holiday nearby at Hot Water Beach. "I like to think that we nearly met lots of times when we were little."

Instead, the couple met and fell in love at university in Auckland five years ago. They often spent summers together at Tairua and when they both finished their Masters studies, they decided it was where they wanted to be.

"Coming back here felt really right," Ryder says. "When I was at university I would come back every weekend to recoup from being in the city. I think it's quite an introverted space, whereas the city is about being more extroverted. Both are satisfying, but I love the space and the emptiness here." Unfortunately, lots of other people like the idea of moving to the Coromandel for the summer and, for a while, it looked like their dream was doomed.

"We had been living at our parents' places and wanted to create our own space together, and we had decided that we would live anywhere as long as we could do that," Ophelia says. "In Tairua, finding a place to live is really about word-of-mouth. Once someone knows you need a house, everyone gets on board to help you. We did start to worry that we would never find anything, especially because it was the start of the summer, but then we found this place."

With three bedrooms, a garage studio for Ryder and a sleep-out that could one day become Ophelia's dedicated workspace, it had all the space they needed. But the joy they felt at finding their house, which is set back from the street by a long driveway and separated from the beach by an empty block of land, helped soften the blow of its shortcomings. "It's an old New Zealand bach that someone had been living in for a while and it needed some love," Ophelia says diplomatically.

Giving the place a good airing out and repainting the interior also helped them feel a lot more positive about moving in. While some aspects of the house are completely beyond their control – "If we owned this house I would rip up the crazy '70s carpet in a second; I feel like I apologise for it every time someone comes over," Ophelia says – they have found clever ways to approach some of the house's more fixable quirks. Ryder has fashioned a leather strap to keep the front door shut, and they've made pulleys to work the light switches. They are both into the same things – some of their own artworks hang on the walls; "amazing, beautiful" chairs made by Ryder sit in the living room; seagrass matting and a few treasured rugs they picked up on holiday in Morocco cover the floors, doing a pretty good job of disguising the carpet.

If we owned this house I would rip up the crazy '70s carpet in a second; I feel like I apologise for it every time someone comes over.

"Because this is the first place we've properly lived in together, we've ended up with a lot of gaps, like I recently realised that we didn't have an iron or an ironing board," Ophelia says. "But we were lucky, because Ryder's parents live down the road and they have given us a lot of cane and bamboo furniture that they brought here when they moved from Hawaii. I'm not sure that we'll always have it, but it really fits here and it's fun to be able to play off the architecture of this house with the things we have been given. We are pretty much on the same wavelength about how we like our space to look."

And outside, they're into the same things as well. They're into their second year of vegetable gardening, hopeful that raised beds and shovelfuls of rich soil will yield a fruitful harvest. Ophelia loves the space and the serenity of their life by the sea, but admits that adapting to the quiet of Tairua took a while. "It's been a big adjustment. Ryder is really good at being by himself, but I have had to adjust to a different way of keeping myself stimulated socially and creatively," she says. "That's been really exciting and good for me, and also a bit challenging. I have missed my girlfriends a lot. I do go up to Auckland often for work, though, and people are always coming to visit. We have put Tairua on the map for a lot of our friends."

Having so much space also means they can run The Afternoon Academy, their free creativity sessions, from home. "It's a series of workshops for kids interested in living a creative life, or who are more interested in art than maths," Ophelia says. "We want to expand their thinking about what art is and the ways of living a creative life. We really wanted to do it in a home setting to show how art and life can overlap, so we work on stuff in our kitchen and in our studios. It's almost like we're just hanging out with them."

Ophelia's own work consists of many strands, all woven together, although she is best known for her distinctive knitted socks. "A lot of my time recently, though, has been spent working on photography projects for New Zealand brands, but in terms of my art practice, I do a lot of drawing."

She and Ryder often work on projects together, and Ophelia says being in Tairua inspires a lot of their work. "Here, we are more acutely aware of nature and the sun rise and set, it gives us more energy and inspiration in our day-to-day lives."

Ryder, she says, is really diligent in his art practice, spending a lot of time in his studio making things, as well as being out and about. "For him it's really important to spend time alone in the ocean. He finds a lot of stillness and peace that helps him in his work." Adds Ryder: "The fact that there's no one around gives you that mental space so you can retreat into yourself. I guess being here offers that potential to me."

While they both daydream about sailing off to other parts of the world one of these days, for now they are more than happy to have made a home of their own by the sea. "We feel really blessed to have a place that we love," Ophelia says. "We are so happy that we found each other early on and that we get to create this life together. We are really thankful for everything that's been and for everything in the future." •

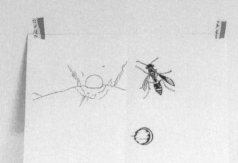

FINISH PROjects
Chateau Marmont
hollywood

Sell chairs MAKE $/get METAL ONE MADE

INVEST INto Ophelia And Frame Her drawing

Buy PLY For prototypes IN thomas?

SEND MARY Story After I Edit

Keep Working IN Studio/Drawing/painting

Continue to chip away at Stone Story

~~Take picture And SEND to S.p~~
get quote   Touch Base With RuFus

~~Get WEBSITE FINished~~

STEVE THANK YOU Letter - Kathy?

PRINT AND Bind thesis - Keri? Ask

8221 SUNSET BOULEVARD HOLLYWOOD CALIFORNIA 90046
TELEPHONE (323) 656-1010 FACSIMILE (323) 655-5311

Alex Bennett & Tina Helm
live with their daughter, Odetta,
& cat, Woody, in Campbells Creek,
Victoria. Alex is a sound engineer;
Tina is an event manager.

WORDS LETA KEENS PHOTOGRAPHS OLGA BENNETT

Like lots of other people, Tina Helm and Alex Bennett had some fairly clear but pretty ambitious ideas of what they wanted to do with their lives. She wanted to run a bed and breakfast and perhaps a café; he wanted to set up a recording studio. They were thinking they might do this in New Zealand, where they were both living at the time. Tina's a Kiwi and Alex had been over there for a few years studying and working in the music studios at Auckland University – but was "ready to get out there and do it rather than be stuck in an institution".

It suddenly clicked, he says, "that my parents had this building with a b&b and space for a studio" back in Australia. Alex and Tina had been together for two or three years at that time, but he'd never really talked about the house in Campbells Creek where he'd spent the first 12 years of his life.

It's a great big rambling joint of a place, spread over about half an acre, with the five-bedroom house, built in the 1850s, incorporating what was once a miners' shop during the Gold Rush (and from which Alex's dad ran an antique store). "My old man's a professional tinkerer," says Alex. "He trained as a scientist, but when he got married, threw in the towel with the career and became a house husband. He restored furniture for the shop, and he'd also buy and sell vintage cars." There are sheds in the grounds where he stored all his wares, plus an old stable that he and Alex's solicitor mum set up as a b&b, another business his dad could run from home. In the '80s, Alex's father and a couple of his mates built a stone barn for his collection of vintage cars. It's where Alex now runs his analogue recording studio, Sound Recordings. "They built a beautiful acoustic space without knowing," he says. "It's the high ceilings and stone walls, plus it's very quiet."

Tina says her first impression of The Diggers' Store, as it is known, was "kind of like a fairytale – I fell in love with it". They found out from Alex's dad when the tenants' lease was up and moved in when Tina was pregnant with Odetta, who's now three.

Alex's family had left Campbells Creek to go to Darwin when his mother got a new job up there. "We were excited about going, but I

do remember my brother and sister and I begging Mum and Dad not to sell the house. At the time, I didn't know why, but maybe I knew I'd come back. Even when we were kids, we could tell it was special."

For Alex, coming back to the family home "was weird, but less weird now – I've got more used to it. There's a lot of the same furniture that was here when I was a kid, and the place still smells the same." Even Tina found it odd at first, "but we've managed to shake out the past and brought our own life into the space."

When Alex's parents bought it, the place was a bit of a dump and needed heaps of work. It had lived numerous lives – for a while it had been a pub; at one time, there was a fruit and vegie shop there; and, in the '50s, it had been left to the Catholic Church, which held services in the shop. After the Bennetts moved to Darwin, various businesses rented the shop and a string of tenants lived in the house.

When Alex and Tina moved in, it was a case of first dusting off years of it being rented out. "None of the tenants really loved it or looked after it," says Alex. He describes it being in a "state of elegant decay". For instance, the roof leaks; there's a danger of the space mural painted on the ceiling in Alex's old bedroom, now the office, being lost. "It's really sad, but I suppose we could always reinstate it," he says.

The part of the five-bedroom house that's most similar to when Alex was a kid is the combined kitchen-dining area – there's a big old fireplace that his dad sometimes used to cook eggs on, with an oven below that is slow enough to dry tomatoes in overnight. The long table, which Alex and Tina retrieved from one of the sheds, is the same one the Bennett family used to sit around years before. "It's crazy, really," says Tina. "A lot of the furniture we're using is stuff Alex's parents stored in the shed, and that was originally in the house when Alex grew up here." The same goes for artwork and a few other bits and pieces – and it's also handy for Odetta, who has an ace collection of vintage toys. "Being related to my father, I could never throw anything away," says Alex. "All my favourite toys are boxed up in the shed – every now and then I have a little dig and find something for her. Some of them I could probably list on eBay!"

Left page, above: Some of the kitchen equipment, including the toaster, was in the house when Alex was a kid.

*If you'd asked me
when I was 14 or
15 and full of angst,
I would never have
wanted to move back
here, but now it's a
perfect place to live.*

←

One of Alex's favourite parts of the dining room is the set of trapdoors his dad put into the ceiling – they can be opened in winter for hot air from the fireplace to heat the two bedrooms directly above. "They're really cool," he says. "When we were kids, we'd look over and drop things down when Mum and Dad were having dinner parties."

He's pretty keen on the two sink units, too – one in the kitchen, one in the dining area. A big Italian family used to live in the house, and the kitchen and dining room hadn't been knocked into one at that stage. "They had two kitchens, and would all eat together on a Sunday. Mum and Dad decided to keep the two sinks – all the crockery and glassware was washed up in one, and the kitchen was for pots and pans. We don't do that, but it's handy when you want a drink."

Early on in Alex and Tina's tenancy, they ran a café in the old shop. It was only open from Friday to Sunday, but they'd be run off their feet. "We'd be flat out, and then spend the whole week prepping," says Alex. It lasted a year, and since then the space has been rented out for poetry nights, workshops, pop-up shops and small weddings, which sometimes flow over to the big room above (originally the Bennett family playroom), which is also sometimes used for exhibitions. Just outside the café and kitchen-dining area is a courtyard Alex and a mate recently paved using old bricks. It's one of Tina's favourite areas, and one that the family spends heaps of time in. "We weren't very good at straight lines and it's subsided here and there," says Alex, "but that's worked in our favour. Everyone says it looks as if it's always been here."

The b&b, again kitted out with bits and bobs from the shed, is on two levels, with the bedroom upstairs in the loft. It hums along nicely, taking far less work than a café, as the couple have discovered. Tina now also has time to manage a local artists' market and

fundraise for a not-for-profit sustainability group, usually working from home. The b&b also ties in well with the studio when recordings stretch over several days, with band members able to roll out of bed and into the studio next door. While his dad used to buy old furniture, Alex, who plays bass in various bands, has combined his interest in music and second-hand by specialising in vintage audio equipment, much of which he picks up on eBay or at op shops.

Sound Recordings is booked out a few days a week, mainly by Melbourne and local musicians, but every now and then "someone with the semblance of a big name" comes along. "I'm lucky, it's working by word of mouth – I've never advertised and my website's terrible," Alex says. His mum "was maybe slightly disappointed" when he moved back to the family home, "because I had been going down the academic route. But now it's fine – she can see we're doing good things and the studio's going really well." His dad, who lives in a new place up the back, is glad to have him home, knowing that he and Tina will look after the place. "If you'd asked me when I was 14 or 15 and full of angst, I would never have wanted to move back here," says Alex, "but now it's a perfect place to live."

Tina had never lived in the country before she moved to Campbells Creek. Three years down the line, she feels "fully immersed in the community. There are lots of like-minded people around our own age, starting their own businesses. Everybody's an artist; everybody's got three year olds."

That helps when you've got a three year old yourself. "If you were going to raise a child in the old way with a village around you, it feels like you've got the village here," says Tina. And the bonus, in this case, is that "Odetta has the opportunity to live in the same place her dad grew up in. That feels very special and old world." •

*Left page, below: Woody
the cat, who Alex and Tina
got from a local shelter,
stretches out in the
courtyard between the
house and the b&b.*

AGNES POTTER WORKS AT ALLPRESS ESPRESSO'S TOKYO ROASTERY AND CAFE.

INTERVIEW DANIELLE DEMETRIOU **PHOTOGRAPHS** GUI MARTINEZ

There is the clean-lined wooden façade, the sliding shutters, the friendly staff and the near-constant aroma of coffee. Allpress Espresso's Tokyo Roastery and Café, housed in a former timber warehouse, has become something of a landmark since opening its doors in the city's low-key Kiyosumi-Shirakawa neighbourhood in August 2014.

A constant stream of customers passes through the doors. They're there to either drink coffee in the frontside café or undergo training next to the roaster behind a double-height wall of glass.

Here, New Zealander Agnes Potter, the general manager, offers a glimpse behind the scenes at Allpress' first Japanese outpost and explains how it all came about.

How did you end up in the coffee industry? I love making coffee and drinking it. But it goes beyond that: I also love the idea of creating an experience for someone – making them feel comfortable while giving them good food and coffee. I've been at Allpress for 10 years – first in Auckland, then London and now Tokyo.

How big is business in Japan? We have about 60 commercial customers, mainly in Tokyo – including Nomu at Nicolai Bergmann and Monocle. Many are also in ski areas – we go to Niseko in Hokkaido, where there are lots of snowboarding Australians and Kiwis, do this mass installation and training and set them all up, and then take everything away again at the end of the season.

How did Allpress end up here? It was the vision of our founder, Michael. He was cycling around the neighbourhood when he saw this building. It was an old timber storage space – there used to be a lot of timber and paper factories in this area. He got off his bike, found the door ajar and looked inside – sunlight was streaming in and he just loved it.

How did he transform it into the current space? It took over a year. To put in a roaster and a café involved lots of regulations, so instead of renovating, we pulled it down, reinforced the foundations and then rebuilt it. It was very important to be respectful of the original architecture and the area. It would have been easier to pull it down and put up a shiny new warehouse, but that's not our style. Instead, we worked with the local architect Taichiro Suzuki and kept a lot of original features. When we close our wooden shutters at night it looks just like the old building.

What other features stand out in the building design? Transparency is important. We have a glass wall between the café and roastery as we want people to see behind the scenes and understand exactly what we do. My favourite spot is on the raised level at the back of the roastery – it gives you the perfect bird's eye view across the roastery and café.

What is unique about Japanese coffee culture? There's a long history of coffee drinking here. There are these old school coffee shops called *kissaten*, where they roast coffee, brew it, then serve it. These people are artisans. Traditionally, it's a very different style of coffee, roasted very darkly, with black beans and an intense flavour.

Left page: Allpress Café and Roastery is in a former timber storage warehouse. It's in a low-key area of Tokyo, which is fast turning into one of the city's coffee hotspots.

Who are your customers in Japan? We get lots of young coffee tourists checking out cool cafés. But there are also lots of quite elderly locals. It's a nice mix. There is one lovely gentleman we call Mister Mister – he's in his 80s in a wheelchair and comes in twice a day for a cappuccino. He sits in front of the coffee machine and chats to the girls. It's become a bit of a community hub here.

What's the biggest differences in terms of other Allpress cafés? The time that people drink coffee here is different. Coffee doesn't seem to be so much of a morning thing – it's more of a late afternoon ritual. We have this crazy busy period between 3 and 5pm.

There are many cult coffee shops in this neighbourhood. Why has it become such a caffeine hotspot? In order to roast coffee you need space – the fact there are many affordable big buildings is probably a factor. And it's an amazing spot, tucked away from the crazy Tokyo action. There are tiny streets, old factories, modern cafés and art galleries. My favourite spots are Kiyosumi Garden and Tomioka Hachiman, a Shinto shrine with an antiques market. The old and the new co-exist really nicely.

How do you see the future of Japan's coffee industry? The specialty coffee industry here is taking off in the same way that it did in the UK maybe seven or eight years ago. I think it's at a really similar stage to the UK at that time. So the really good cafés are still few and far between – and I think we're going to start seeing that change really quickly now that there's a bit of momentum.

What's your vision for Allpress in Japan? The things that we value most are sincerity and being generous of spirit. We don't have an end goal in mind, we just want to keep doing what we've always done around the world – that's supply lots of great coffee and help customers create thriving businesses.

What is special about the way Allpress make their coffee? The way we roast it is different, it's called hot air roasting. The coffee beans are suspended on a stream of fluidised air – that means it doesn't come into contact with the side of the roaster so you don't get burning or scorching. It also removes smoke from the chamber. It creates a much cleaner and sweeter flavour quality, which is different from a traditional drum roasting technique.

How has the transition been moving from London to Japan? When they asked me if I'd be willing to move to Japan, I was a bit shocked at first and thought, "No way, I don't speak Japanese!" But I've always had a bit of a fascination with Japanese culture and I'd visited a few times and really enjoyed it. The more I thought about it, the more I realised it would be a really interesting experience.

What do you enjoy most about working here? I live about 15 minutes away by bike. I love cycling around this city, it's the nicest commute.

Biggest challenges? For me, the language is challenging. But the culture is probably even more so in some ways. It's really different. We probably have a slightly less formal and more simple approach to business, which is not necessarily the norm in Japan.

But it's great and I see new things and meet new people every day. Our customers are starting to get to know us. We're really respectful of the culture here, but we're also bringing our own culture as well. •

Left page: The neighbourhood of Kiyosumi-Shirakawa is a mix of cool cafés and art galleries with old factories, traditional gardens and shrines.

FIND YOUR NEAREST ALLPRESS CAFÉ

*Allpress currently roasts in Auckland, Dunedin, Sydney, Melbourne, London and Tokyo. The Allpress Café finder app, for iPhone and Android, will help lead you to the best coffee in town. For more information, visit **allpressespresso.com***

LY YEOW LIVES IN SINGAPORE WITH HER PARENTS & BROTHER, KEVIN. SHE IS AN ARTIST.

INTERVIEW LETA KEENS **PHOTOGRAPHS** ELVINA FARKAS

Where do you live? I live with my mum and dad and brother in a five-room flat. My parents bought this place almost 30 years ago when it was new. My brother was five at that time and lived at the office my dad and mum ran – my mum and brother slept on the sofa and my dad slept on the reclining chair every night. I got lucky, I've lived in this house since I was born. I studied in Sydney for about three years, and missed this space every day. Singapore is really fast paced and things change rapidly. But in this neighbourhood, changes happen slowly. One of my favourite stalls downstairs has chicken rice. The auntie has worked there for as long as I can remember, and I've ordered the same dish for 20 years.

What are your neighbours like? Our neighbours opposite used to have a chihuahua that barked every time she saw me, maybe because I've always preferred cats. Our neighbours on the left have been here as long as we have – they used to hear me crying as a kid whenever Mum left for work. Our neighbour upstairs is a beautician, so we used to go up there for cheap facial sessions. Another auntie on the fifth floor delivers cultured milk drinks to our doorstep. She's also a pretty good tailor who works from home and has altered many of our dresses.

How long have you had your room? My brother and I used to share it, but we were always at each other's throats. When I was in primary school, he moved to the room next door. The house has been more peaceful ever since, which my mum greatly appreciates.

What can you see from your room? All my friends say we have the best view. We see the train winding through, the water in the nearby reservoir, lots of greenery, and sunsets. I go to sleep to the sound of crickets and wake up to the beautiful chirping of birds. We have no idea when the spaces before us will get developed into high-rise buildings, so we'll enjoy the view while it lasts.

What kind of work do you do? My dream was to be an artist when I was young, and I'm still trying to stay afloat on the same path. I majored in jewellery and textiles at the University of New South Wales, but when I got my heart really broken in my 20s, I started drawing and found it to be very therapeutic. Drawing is a voice for those feelings I cannot articulate. My first exhibition, *Catboy*, held in 2014, was inspired by this heartbreak.

Commercially, I have done projects for Airbnb, painted murals for Starbucks and done chalkboard art for some cafés in Singapore. Currently, I am working on many of my own projects, including a series of postcards called *Today I Will*, with illustrations and daily reminders of positivity, optimism and mindfulness.

←

Have you always been into art?
I've loved it since I was young.
I would cut up scraps of cloth and
staple them into dresses for my
Barbie dolls. I used to doodle on
the furniture and walls, too, and
often got punished. Thankfully,
I've managed to find a secret spot
under the bed frame to doodle on
– my mum hasn't noticed.

What's it like working from home?
It means sometimes I roll out of
bed and start drawing in pyjamas.
It's also really comfortable to enjoy
the silence at night, drawing when
everybody in the house is asleep.
I feel relaxed most of the time when
I am working on my personal projects,
but it can get stressful when I am
working on commercial projects
because my brain is in overdrive
until the work gets completed.

**Where does all the stuff in your
room come from?** Where do I start!
I salvage bits and pieces that speak to
me. I have many things up on my wall,
including postcards from friends,
drawings I have done and reminders
to better myself. I also have a plastic
lid with a cute polar bear illustration
on the wall – it's from an ice cream
I shared with my boyfriend when we
were travelling in Naoshima (Japan).
There is a picture by my bed with the
line 'Wild at Heart'. It was hanging
in the changing room of a vintage
dress shop; I loved the words so much
and asked if I could take it. The
vintage cases are from flea markets
in New Zealand and Australia.

There are so many little bottles
filled with my stone collections,
flowers, pinecones and seeds from
plants I don't even recognise but
found interesting. I recently brought

home some honesty flowers – I first
saw these flowers in New Zealand,
and have been on the lookout for them
ever since. A few months ago, when
I was travelling in Austria, I spotted
them in a house down the street from
our Airbnb apartment. The owner
was Romanian, so we communicated
mostly through hand gestures and
shared laughter as she cut off a stem
of flowers for me to bring back home.
Such keepsakes are inexpensive
but extremely valuable to me.

What are your favourite pieces?
I really love to collect stones. The
ones picked from the ice glacier in
New Zealand shimmer silver glitter
under sunlight. Those collected
in Taiwan are round and smooth,
sometimes with natural patterns
of white lines cutting through like
an abstract painting. Stones from
the Great Ocean Road are really flat
and I drew faces on each of them.
My favourite of all is a white petoskey
stone picked from the beach on Lanyu
Island (Taiwan), weathered through
all its journeys into a beautiful oval.
These treasures are reminders of
times spent near the sea. The process
of picking them is a chance encounter;
you never know what kind of rocks you
will find, and the ones we pick will
always be special.

**Is there organisation amid all the
clutter in your room?** Definitely!
All my collections are in their
respective bottles, and I know exactly
where the paper and markers are
stored. Boxes are used to contain my
letters; necklaces are hung loosely on
a twisted paper clip acting as a hook.
My badges are pinned onto a cloth
hanging over my Mac, a full display
for easy pairing to the daily outfit.
I would call it organised chaos!

*Left page, below right:
Ly Yeow's belongings
have spilt over into the
living room.*

Above: The only time Ly Yeow gets to cook is late at night, after her mum has gone to bed.

What are you like with the cleaning? We do have a part-time helper who comes in once a week and helps out with most cleaning. My drawing table is an important space for myself where I spend most of my time. Even on late nights, I keep my drawing desk organised and clean after use.

What kind of things do you need to have around you? My happiness is dependent on the amount of morning light that seeps in through the windows, so the curtains are kept open when I sleep. I always need my sketchbook and brush pens around – I need to draw every day. It's like a voice for me to express myself and my reason to breathe. A bottle of water is always placed on the table, too – best to keep hydrated at all times!

Your belongings seem to have escaped from your room – what do your parents think about that? My things have spilt into the living room – I have too many art materials. They're in shelves that were given to me by a friend. I have also taken over the kitchen; there are actually multiple shelves and extra cabinets with my kitchenware and bakeware. I cannot stop buying plates and spoons, especially if they are made of wood. My parents are generally OK with additions in the living room, but Mum is not pleased with the extra junk in her kitchen. Like all mums, the kitchen is a sacred place. The only way to resolve this is to bake late at night when she is asleep.

You've just got engaged, so you'll be moving out soon. What will your new place be like? My fiancé and I are homebodies. He loves his man cave, and I love my little hole. Building a new life together and leaving our comfort spaces is going to be challenging. We've bought a 40-year-old apartment with terrazzo flooring, and have started buying pre-loved furniture. Soon, it will be filled with wood elements and a lot of plants. We need a huge wall to put up all the paintings I've drawn of us. We will also have a huge dining table that will function as an art studio when I start teaching little ones at home. We have a spacious kitchen and I cannot wait to start baking – let the aroma of cake fill up our home! •

JAE-SUN YOU LIVES IN SEOUL WITH J,
HIS PERSIAN CAT. JAE-SUN IS A DESIGNER
& HAS A SHOP.

WORDS GEMINI KIM & LETA KEENS **PHOTOGRAPHS** SUK KUHN OH

The best thing about Jae-sun You's apartment, he reckons, is the view. "It's on top of a hill, and looks out over the mountains and the Seoul Tower." He's been there for eight or nine years and, at first, didn't think he needed too much else. When he and J, his Chinchilla Persian cat, moved in, he was determined to leave the place bare.

Jae-sun's life in his five-year-old shop revolves around a hotchpotch of stuff, and he wanted home life to be the opposite. "My home was only for rest – I don't cook or do any special home things there. My friends don't visit. Only necessary things were allowed there."

It didn't take long to ditch the minimal look, and for vintage bits and bobs to sneak into his little three-room flat, which is about 20 minutes' walk from his shop. The sofa and every shelf is now inhabited by old toys – a cabinet, which Jae-sun calls his "treasure box", is stuffed full of dolls. "Initially, it was in my shop, and filled with not-for-sale items." To save customers the disappointment of walking away empty-handed, it seemed easier to bring it home. "It was very hard for me to tell them they couldn't buy the dolls," he says.

He tries not to shift things around too much at home: "I just move things from my shop to my flat." Sometimes it's because he's gone overboard on stock for the shop, and doesn't have

the room for it there; otherwise there are pieces friends have picked up on their travels, or things he has unearthed along the way. "I'm a scavenger – it is part of my life, collecting things from the streets," he says. "Lampshades, wardrobes, I got them all from there."

Jae-sun, whose only concession to the new is in what he wears ("vintage clothes don't suit me"), has been into second-hand since he finished uni. "That was the first time I'd visited Tokyo," he says. "I came across a vintage shop at the end of an alley in Shimokitazawa that had lots of dolls. I couldn't help falling in love with them – they were the cutest things I'd ever seen."

Part of the appeal, he says, is that each has a story. "Some of the faces had been spoilt – maybe the first owners had treated them roughly. I liked the fact that they were hurt and not brand new – each one was totally unique, like a human."

Until recently, Jae-sun's working hours were from about 10.30 in the morning to 11.30 at night, "but my 13-year-old flatmate isn't feeling very well these days, so I try to come home by about 8. I still have the same workload, though, so have no choice but to work from home. Unexpectedly, I'm finding I can concentrate more on drawing at home than I do at the workshop – that might be because I have a cat on my knees."

For most of the day, Jae-sun is holed up in his shop, Goyang-yi Samchon, which translates as Uncle Cat, a nickname given to him by one of his nieces. Every cat feels like a friend, he says. "I've loved cats since I was a child. I grew up in the countryside and used to feed the cats that lived around my house."

Most of the things in the shop are designed and made by Jae-sun. He usually starts by doing watercolour paintings of cats, which he then has printed onto fabrics and paper to make hundreds of different items, including cushions, dolls and stationery. "I make my own cat characters and blend them with the vintage mood I've always loved," he says. "Some of my inspiration comes from old paper dolls I've collected, and I also use old magazines and fabrics as inspiration, as well as old buildings, signs, bricks and windows – they're all so lovely. Many of them aren't the usual things you'd be inspired by, but when I see them, I can't wait to mingle them with my cat illustrations. Most of the cat faces are either J or my friends' cats. I want them to look as lifelike as possible, so I use photos."

As well as his own cat creations, he is also surrounded by a number of vintage pieces. "For a long time I was collecting only American or Japanese vintage goods, but I recently got hooked on Korean pieces, especially from the early 20th century, such as the old pharmacy bench that I now have in the shop. It is almost impossible to find things like that – they're not in pharmacies anymore, even in the countryside, and you barely ever see them in vintage markets. When I came across this one, I didn't hesitate to buy it."

The shop, which is divided into a workshop and the showroom, is in a converted church. "There's a steeple on the rooftop and an old wooden staircase which I really liked," says Jae-sun. As well, all the windows look out onto the ginkgo trees that turn yellow in autumn.

Goyang-yi Samchon is one floor above street level, in rooms that were once rented out to web designers. "I was only looking for somewhere on the first floor, not only because of the cheap rent but also because I hoped it would be a hidden, secret shop that only a few people knew." Hong-dae, the neighbourhood it is in, is full of restaurants, cafés and galleries. "There are also lots of other workrooms and fancy goods stores as well – it's filled with things that stimulate me, and make me want to stay here."

The shop is only open on Fridays and Saturdays, but Jae-sun, who wouldn't mind owning a café, is there the rest of the week in the workshop, sewing and doing all the other things involved in the business. "I enjoy making fabric objects," says Jae-sun. "I'm trying to learn more about making bags. At the moment I'm making one tote bag a day, it is so exciting."

He's quite happy to sell his bags, but isn't always so thrilled when some other pieces get sold, especially if they're vintage. "Sometimes, people buy my favourite pieces when I'm not quite ready to let them go," he says. "I feel very sorry then." •

NATALY LEE & EUAN GRAY LIVE IN PHNOM PENH.
SHE IS A DESIGNER & PHOTOGRAPHER; HE IS A
JAZZ MUSICIAN & PRODUCER.

WORDS KOREN HELBIG **PHOTOGRAPHS** NATALY LEE
PORTRAIT CORINNE TAN

The concept of home can be a tad complicated when your roots are firmly entwined within two wildly different cultures. Take Nataly Lee, who grew up in Wellington and then Brisbane, but was born in Cambodia. In 1984, when Nataly was just 11 months old, her parents fled their homeland, walking to a Thai refugee camp to escape the brutal guerrilla warfare engulfing Cambodia. "Growing up, I always felt like I was really Khmer, really Cambodian," Nataly says. "But it was only once I got to Cambodia that I realised I'm actually really Australian." She first returned to Cambodia as an 18 year old and was shocked to discover the conditions much of her extended family was living in: "I think I cried every night." Yet she somehow felt instantly at home, too, as if she belonged amid this sweaty non-stop hustle and bustle. Still, another decade would pass before Nataly would give Cambodian living a real go.

In the meantime, she met jazz musician and producer Euan Gray (they married in 2013) and shared a succession of Brisbane rentals, each decked out with a growing mix of furniture and trinkets Nataly scored free from photo shoots, as her work as a magazine stylist and fashion director began to pick up speed. In 2007, the couple visited Cambodia together for the first time. "I hadn't really heard about Cambodia before I met Nat, except for the Pol Pot regime on television, so it was a bit of a mystery," says Euan. They both loved it so much they began making the 6750-kilometre trip north for a month each year.

By 2011 the couple had moved over more permanently, but still felt torn between the two countries. Returning to Brisbane for a year in 2014 crystallised everything: it was time to commit to Cambodia. That meant finding a rental they could feel at home in. "Houses here are usually fully furnished, so you get stuck with this horrendous, cheap Chinese furniture," says Nataly. "And a lot of places look like giant bathrooms because they put tiles on the walls to shoulder level so it's easier to clean. Houses here are very functional, not aesthetically pleasing."

Luck struck when Nataly got in touch with a local architect she'd previously worked for, who was looking to renovate a derelict two-storey house in Phnom Penh's fancy Boeung Keng Kang 1 area. "It's the nicest part of Phnom Penh," says Nataly. "There are wide streets, trees and a lot of NGOs and businesses, so it feels very safe." The downside is that rental prices are usually really high – for Cambodia, at least – but Nataly settled on a sweet deal: in return for cheaper rent, she'd design and style her whole flat, and cast a creative eye over the block's other three apartments, too. "He gave me full creative control," she says.

Nataly started with blank walls, freshly laid concrete floors and floor-to-ceiling windows. She set out to create a retreat from the chaos of the concrete jungle outside. Says Euan: "On the street and in people's houses, there's an aesthetically oppressive, aggressive kind of vibe. It doesn't really reflect in the people; they're lovely and warm and friendly. We've always wanted sanctuaries in this place and Nat's been great at creating that. We have a Zen kind of feeling, which juxtaposes with the outside world, so it's a relief to come home."

The apartment has two bedrooms, which sit over a large, rectangular, open-plan kitchen and living area. Nataly's mum occupies one of those bedrooms, dividing her time between Australia and Cambodia. Nataly even designed the furniture herself. "If there was one word to describe interior decorating here in Cambodia, it would be 'creativity'," Nataly says. "Because there's no Ikea or proper op shops, you have to really search or get creative and design your own." Her collection of cushions is another reflection of that creativity; they're examples of designs Nataly handmade for her homewares label SAAT, which means 'beautiful' in Khmer.

The former driveway has been converted into Nataly's studio, a greenhouse-like cube. It does get pretty steamy in there at times, but that's a price she's happy to pay for an unending stream of natural light. She initially dreamed of opening a little café there for her mum to run, but instead went for a studio as her work as a designer, creative director and photographer gained traction. It's naturally morphed into a co-working space for local creatives, and Nataly plonked a 3.5 metre table in the centre to encourage gatherings. "I've grown a five-metre vertical garden behind the studio, which is now really lush and beautiful," Nataly says. "Living in Australia we were so connected to nature and had such access to it. I wanted to bring that to our environment here."

The newest addition to their digs is a piano, which had to be crane-lifted into the house through a window. "Four years ago, we would never have been able to get a real piano that could be tuned," says Euan. "But now one of my best friends has a piano shop and they just loaded it in: eight dudes, 20 minutes." The apartment walls are thin and Euan's sure their neighbours hear every note, just as the roaring of motorbikes outside often filters in. "It's hard to get a quiet space in Cambodia so we've just submitted to being acoustically porous to the outside world," Euan says. "Though there's a nightclub not far away that I would happily burn down."

While the apartment's aesthetic is a departure from the usual Cambodian style, the odd nod to Khmer culture does feature. Rattan mats give the concrete floors a warmer feel and a little Buddha statue sits high above their staircase. "That's really important to Mum," Nataly says. "In Cambodia, a lot of the buildings have spirit houses to make peace with any floating spirits that may reside on the property, so they don't bring bad energy to your space." The place is also dotted with photos from the pair's 2013 wedding, a two-day affair in the Cambodian coastal province of Kep, which merged Nataly and Euan's histories: they kicked off with a brilliantly coloured Khmer ceremony, then celebrated on the second day with a white-gown-and-fancy-suit Australian service.

That ability to blend Khmer and Aussie culture is perhaps the hallmark of Nataly and Euan's relationship and their home. At their table, for example, Nataly might dish up traditional Cambodian amok – cubes of fish, coconut cream and leafy greens wrapped in banana leaves – but tea might later be served in the pot Euan's grandmother received as a wedding gift, which the pair safely carried all the way from Scotland. They love moving freely between these two worlds, and creating a home that incorporates the best bits of the two countries they adore. "For me, a space is so important. It's the place you spend most of your time, where you can reflect on your day, so it's important that it's nice," Nataly says. "When I design spaces, it's not so much for what it looks like, but what it feels like. Our house feels unique. We think it's one of a kind." •

AZUMI SAKATA LIVES IN SENDAGI, TOKYO. SHE IS AN ARTIST & ART TEACHER.

INTERVIEW DANIELLE DEMETRIOU **PHOTOGRAPHS** BENJAMIN HOSKING

How did you end up living in Sendagi? I used to work in an art gallery here as a student and always wanted to live here. It has a very old Japanese feel. There are many houses where writers and artists lived in the past. There are a lot of temples and graveyards. It's like an old art town. Atmospheric and historic. Since Japan's 2011 earthquake, it has started changing – people have been pulling down more old buildings and putting up new ones. But it is still an interesting area.

What about the building itself? It was built in 1994 by the owner, who is an architect. There are only three properties in the building – an office on the ground floor and a young woman on the first floor who I don't really know. I'm on the top floor.

What do you love most about your apartment? It's quite small – about 40 square metres – and it's along a big road so it's a bit noisy, plus there's not much natural sunlight. But I loved the high ceilings. That's what initially attracted me. I do believe in love at first sight in terms of buildings. You have to trust your gut instincts in these situations.

How would you describe your interior style? I'm not a minimalist. For me, it's very comfortable – but for others, it might be a bit scary at times. I love travelling and have collected many things from trips. For example, there is this soft hand-knitted toy which a friend in London bought for me from a charity shop about 20 years ago, when I was studying there. I was always fascinated with London charity shops. It's got really unusual blue eyes plus different length legs. I can't imagine who made it – maybe a child? It's one of my treasures.

Any other examples of treasured items? I'm really interested in these old religious artefacts called ex voto – they are used among Catholics in Latin America. So if someone has an injured hand, they would buy a wooden hand and make it an offering at church. My friend's grandmother in England used to collect them and gave me one.

Can you tell us about your work? I'm an art teacher and I am an artist. I work mainly with cloth and embroidery. I used to focus on etching, but as a child, I always liked cloth and fabrics – I've now gone back to my roots by working with cloth.

Why do you like working with fabric? I like the texture and the way it feels. When I'm sewing, it's like a form of meditation for me. I also draw and paint. I recently had an exhibition and made tiny pillows and cushions. There was an installation with a bed and I stacked up the little pillows on top. Many times, I've been told I could mass produce my work in factories, but I don't want to. For me, this meditation time is important. I want to do this by hand myself. That's the whole point.

Left page, top left:
A friend bought
Azumi the blue
doll at a charity
shop in London.

How did your childhood influence your creative path? I grew up in Kanagawa prefecture not far from Tokyo. My mother used to make clothes and do embroidery. She also made these metalwork enamel items using quite a difficult technique known as *shippo-yaki* (cloisonné). My father is an office worker but also published origami books and taught origami in his spare time. So they were both fairly creative.

What do you think your work says about you? I'm interested in what I cannot see. For example, what happens after death. I'm not religious myself but I am fascinated by the different belief systems of other people. At the moment, I'm looking into ancient Egyptian beliefs in terms of what they thought happened after death. So I'm making mummies these days.

Why the fascination with religious beliefs? What enchants me is that thousands of years after the ancient Egyptians created a whole belief system around death – with all these curses and charms to make the dead happy in the afterlife – science still cannot understand death. That's what makes it interesting to me.

The atmosphere in your apartment is quite light – how do you balance out your interests in faith and death with the lighter side of life? I have lots of green plants – mainly from my parents – and also I love flowers, such as the dark red dahlias I have here now. They are currently in season so are beautiful. In general, I also like things that are very unique and make me laugh, such as my David Shrigley picture, with the elephant standing on a car.

What is it like living and working in the same space? It can go both ways, good and bad. I wake up in the morning and I can see straightaway what I made the day before – it's a good way to see whether I like something or not. The cons would be that my life gets consumed with work at times. Boundaries are difficult. As much as I love my work, it can be a tough, agonising process at times – creating something from nothing.

What do you do when you're not working? I'm always thinking about work. But when I'm not, I suppose I would go out drinking with friends. Or cook Portuguese food at home for friends. I love Portuguese food – my favourite things to make are pork and clam dishes and soups.

Are you usually at your desk? Yes, I spend most of my time working at the desk. When I'm doing big drawings or paintings, I often clear the space in the back by the kitchen and work there.

Would you say you are messy? I'm average, I suppose. When I'm doing big scale drawings, it can get quite messy everywhere. Or when I'm using the sewing machine and there's lots of fabric lying around. I'm not the tidiest person – I'm quite normal I think. •

JORDAN MARZUKI LIVES & WORKS IN JAKARTA. HE IS A DESIGNER & CO-FOUNDER OF THE BALLETCATS.

WORDS LETA KEENS **PHOTOGRAPHS** MUHAMMAD FADLI

Jordan Marzuki specialises in the odd and unexpected in his slightly deranged label, The Balletcats – tote bags and sweatshirts with illustrations of dissected cats, rifle-wielding moggies, and felines wearing human stoles; an action figure of a boy, ribs exposed, with a cat down his shorts.

It seems just right, then, that every now and then a giant lizard slithers through the house he shares with his architect father, Pris, and three cats. Or that there's an occasional visit from "some kind of stinky animal – what's it called, a skunk. We're sitting on the edge of a swamp and have almost everything here in the way of wildlife".

The Marzuki family had been living on the outskirts of Jakarta for 15 years before knocking down their house and building a new one. Jordan felt sad, he says, to see the old place demolished, "but excited as well. It was a collaboration between me and my mother and father. We thought it would be good if we could make somewhere for my father to work after he retired. And my mother had always wanted an open space with good circulation of air."

Sadly, Jordan's mum died two years ago, so she didn't have much of a chance to enjoy the new house. And Jordan's dad doesn't get to spend much time there now – he's still going to his office every day. "If you work outside the home, you can spend two or three hours a day travelling because of the traffic."

Jordan, who studied in Jakarta and Switzerland, usually has the place to himself. As soon as it was built, he gave up working at a design firm and set up his office at home. "It's so unproductive commuting in Jakarta," he says. "I know I'm putting an emphasis on traffic jams, but that's how it is here. I also like the fact that if I've finished some work, I can go to my bed for five or 10 minutes."

And that's only a step or two from his work area – his part of the house consists of one room with a mezzanine level. His bed is at one end of the room; desks, designed by his father and made locally, are at the other, and in between are shelves full of his stuff. "It's basically a one-stop service for living," he says. "You can sleep here, you can work here, you can do anything here." When clients visit, Jordan says, "I remove the bed. I want to move all my personal stuff up into the mezzanine level, but at the moment that's used for storage."

The lack of storage is one of the few complaints Jordan has about the place. "My father didn't want any closed or isolated areas. I wanted him to build a storage room, but he decided not to. I have to put my Balletcats stock in the guest room and anywhere I can, and sometimes I get very irritated at how messy it looks."

←

Jordan set up The Balletcats (named after an unusual pose struck by one of his cats) in 2008 with his girlfriend, Fatriana Zukhra, both students at the time. She now comes over to his place every weekend "to brainstorm – she's involved in all the work I do". Balletcats, he says, "is my statement to humanity about how I hate people being bad to animals and nature". In spite of rifle-wielding cats, he tries not to hit the audience over the head with a sledgehammer. "I want it to be very subtle so people don't notice there's a statement there at all."

Over the years, Balletcats continued partly as an antidote to some of the less appealing work he had to do as a graphic designer. "I was working at an office five days a week and was overworked and underappreciated," he says. "The worst client was a real estate company – most of the work was for that kind of commercial culture. Balletcats was my side job to keep me sane."

These days, Jordan, who describes himself as a multi-disciplinary designer, works on books and freelance fashion design, "and I'm starting to be serious on film-making. I've also got a children's book coming up. It's a mishmash – if I feel like doing it, I do it. But no real estate anymore."

Apart from Jordan's room, the house is calmly minimal: "That's my dad's

look – he doesn't buy trinkets, he never buys decoration for the house, he's very Indonesian in his style and the way he organises things." Jordan's look, on the other hand, is "more a cabinet of curiosities".

Even as a kid, he says, his room was "kind of messy" and he reckons he got his love of having lots of stuff around him from his mother, "who always bought me things for my room when she travelled". It's when he's travelling himself that he picks up most of his bits and bobs, including medical paraphernalia. "I like to visit thrift shops and off-the-beaten track stores around the world," he says. "Every time I travel I manage to buy masks and other things – I wouldn't say I like creepy stuff, but I do like to buy things with faces."

He also picks up a stack of books wherever he goes. "I like to buy foreign language books that I don't understand – I go to lots of second-hand bookshops. I like children's books that are really really bad – politically incorrect ones with lots of violence."

His bookshelves, stuffed with all his offbeat books, "are one of the reasons I like to be here – they keep me inspired. I think I'll stop buying trinkets, because it's starting to get dusty in here. My dad's much better at cleaning than me, I'm sorry to say, and I never let him in here." •

Previous page, left: Jordan's dad, Fris, works at a bench in the kitchen. Left page, above left: Jordan with his girlfriend and Balletcats co-founder Fatriana Zukhra. Above right: Jordan with his cat Glunyu.